DWELL DEEP

OR, HILDA THORN'S LIFE STORY

AMY LE FEUVRE

1ˢᵗ WORLD
LIBRARY
Literary Society

Dwell Deep

Amy Le Feuvre

© 1st World Library, 2009
PO Box 2211
Fairfield, IA 52556
www.1stworldlibrary.com
First Edition

LCCN: 2009923345

Softcover ISBN: 978-1-4218-8805-7
Hardcover ISBN: 978-1-4218-8904-7
eBook ISBN: 978-1-4218-8706-7

Purchase *"Dwell Deep"*
as a traditional bound book at:
www.1stWorldLibrary.com/purchase.asp?ISBN=978-1-4218-8805-7

1st World Library is a literary, educational organization
dedicated to:

- Creating a free internet library of downloadable ebooks

- Hosting writing competitions and offering book publishing
scholarships.

1st World Library Literary Society

Giving Back to the World

"If you want to work on the core problem, it's early school literacy."

- James Barksdale, former CEO of Netscape

"No skill is more crucial to the future of a child, or to a democratic and prosperous society, than literacy."

- Los Angeles Times

"Literacy... means far more than learning how to read and write... The aim is to transmit... knowledge and promote social participation."

- UNESCO

"Literacy is not a luxury, it is a right and a responsibility. If our world is to meet the challenges of the twenty-first century we must harness the energy and creativity of all our citizens."

- President Bill Clinton

"Parents should be encouraged to read to their children, and teachers should be equipped with all available techniques for teaching literacy, so the varying needs and capacities of individual kids can be taken into account."

- Hugh Mackay

CONTENTS

CHAPTER I

A NEW HOME

'Meet is it changes should control
Our being, lest we rust in ease.'
                              —*Tennyson*

A golden cornfield in the still sunshine of a warm August afternoon. In one corner of it, bordering a green lane, a group of shady elms, and under their shadow a figure of a young girl, who, gazing dreamily before her, sat leaning her head against an old gnarled trunk in quiet content. A small-shaped head, with dark curly hair, and a pair of blue-grey eyes with black curved lashes, these were perhaps her chief characteristics; more I cannot say, for it is difficult to describe oneself, and it was I, Hilda Thorn, who was seated there.

It was a beautiful scene before me. Beyond the corn stretched a green valley, and far in the distance were blue misty hills and moorland. My soul seemed rested by the sweet stillness around, but from the beauties of nature my eyes kept reverting to the Bible on my knee, and two words on the open page were occupying my thoughts—'Dwell deep.'

I had been left an orphan at the age of ten, both parents dying in India whilst I was at an English boarding-school. There I stayed till I was nineteen, when I went to an old cousin in London, and for three years I lived a quiet uneventful life in a dull London square, seeing very little society but that of elderly ladies and a few clergymen.

Suddenly my whole life was changed. My guardian, who had been living abroad with his wife and family, returned to England, and wished me to make my home with him. And my cousin was quite willing that it should be so.

'You are young, my dear,' she said to me, 'and it is only right for you to mix with young people and see the world. I am getting to prefer being alone, so I shall not miss you.'

It did not take long to settle matters, and I soon left London for my guardian's lovely place in Hertfordshire, feeling both shy and curious at the strange future before me.

But during my stay in London there had been another and perhaps a greater change in my life than this. I had been brought up religiously, had said my prayers night and morning, and had read my Bible regularly once a day, but with these outward forms my religion ceased.

I suppose all my thoughts were in the world and of the world. I had been a favourite with my school-fellows, who assured me I had more than my fair share of beauty, and with all the ignorance and inexperience of girlhood had planned out glowing descriptions of the brilliant offers of marriage I would have, and the delightful times before me. I listened and laughed at them, yet had chafed at the quiet monotony of my cousin's home, and had longed for a break to come in the dull routine of our daily life.

Then one night I had attended some mission services that

Amy Le Feuvre

were held in our church, and for the first time beheld life and death as they are in reality. For several days I was in great distress of mind, and turned with real earnestness to my Bible for guidance and comfort. The light came at last, and I saw how completely Christ had taken my place as a sinner, and how as a little child I must come and claim the pardon that He had died to procure, and was now holding out to me as a free gift.

This brought a wonderful joy into my life, and as each day seemed to draw me nearer to my Saviour, I felt that no life could be monotonous with all the boundless opportunities of speaking and working for Him. My craving for a gay, worldly life passed away, and a deep, restful peace crept into my heart and remained there.

When I told my cousin of my experience she looked puzzled, and shook her head.

'Young people nowadays always go to such extremes; but you look happy, child, and I shall not interfere with your serious views.'

And then my guardian arrived on the scene—a tall, stern-looking man, with iron-grey hair. He had just retired from an Indian cavalry regiment, and still bore upon him the stamp of an officer accustomed to command.

He only stayed with us a few days, and then carried me off to his country home. It all seemed very strange to me, and, though Mrs. Forsyth gave me a warm welcome, I could see I was an object of curiosity and criticism on the part of her three daughters, who were all lively, talkative girls. Two grown-up sons completed the home circle, both of whom seemed to be at home doing nothing. I learnt afterwards that Hugh, the eldest, wrote a great deal for some scientific magazines, and was up in London very constantly engaged in literary pursuits.

My thoughts were perplexed and anxious as I laid my head down on my pillow the first night. Little as I had as yet seen of them, I knew from the conversation around me that there was no one who would sympathise with me in religious matters. How should I, a mere beginner in the Christian life, be able to take a stand amongst this happy, careless family circle, who already were including me in dances and theatricals that were shortly coming off in the neighbourhood? And then the next afternoon, pleading fatigue from my journey, I saw the girls go off to a tennis party with their mother and, taking my Bible in hand, crept out of the house and grounds, and found my way, as I have already mentioned, into that quiet, sunshiny cornfield.

Was it by chance that my eyes alighted on those two little words in Jeremiah? I think not. I had heard a sermon upon them, and now I seized hold of them with a fresh realization of their strength and beauty.

'Dwell deep!' Oh, how I silently prayed, as I sat there looking up into the bright blue above me, that I might do so day by day and hour by hour! Silently could I feast and refresh my soul, even amidst the gay laughter and talk around me, for had I not an unseen Friend always with me, upon whom I could lean for support and guidance through every detail in my daily life?

And so I sat on, drinking in the sweet, fresh country air, and feeling so thankful for the quiet time I was having.

Suddenly the barking of a dog and men's voices roused me from my meditations, and in another moment Kenneth Forsyth sprang over a stile near, and approached me, in company with another young fellow about the same age.

'Halloo!' was his exclamation as he perceived me; 'is it you, Miss Thorn? And all by yourself, too? What a shame of the girls! Let me introduce my friend, Captain Gates. You certainly have selected a cool spot. May we share your retreat? We were just lamenting the heat, and longing for a piece of shade.'

And, without waiting for my answer, he flung himself down on the grass beside me, whilst Captain Gates lounged against a tree close by.

I was a little vexed at the interruption, and did not feel inclined to stay there with them. Kenneth was at present almost a stranger to me. He had a mischievous, quizzical intonation in his voice when he spoke to me, and Violet, his youngest sister, a bright, merry schoolgirl of fourteen, had confided in me the previous night that 'Kenneth was never so happy as when he was teasing people, and that he took stock of every one, and mimicked them—very often to their faces.'

I closed my little Bible quietly. My first impulse had been to hide it, but I conquered that as being unworthy of a Christian, and then I said brightly,—

'I have enjoyed this so much. You don't know what a pleasure it is, after the grime and smoke and roar of London, to come to a place like this. Your sisters wanted me to go with them this afternoon, but I was a little tired, so came out here instead.'

'And are you fond of solitude?' inquired Captain Gates. 'Most girls are not, I fancy.'

'I like it—sometimes,' I replied slowly.

'This afternoon, for instance,' Kenneth said, with a laugh. 'But too much solitude is bad for the young, so we are breaking in upon it for a good purpose. It makes them morbid and self-engrossed.'

I saw that his quick eyes had already noted my Bible, and was vexed to feel my cheeks flushing.

'Miss Thorn's appearance is certainly not morbid,' said Captain Gates good-naturedly; and as I looked up at him I met a frank, kindly glance from his dark eyes.

'No, I am not morbid,' I said; 'I am very happy.'

'Ah!' put in Kenneth with a mock sigh, 'you are looking out at life with inexperienced eyes at present, and everything has a roseate hue to you. Your experience has yet to come!'

For some little time longer they stayed there with me laughing and talking, and then we all went back to the house together, and my quiet time was over. I liked Kenneth better than his brother Hugh, who seemed to me to be too sarcastic and supercilious for any one to be comfortable in his presence; but there was a look of mischief in Kenneth's eyes which puzzled me, as again and again this afternoon his glance met mine.

At dinner I was enlightened. It was a merry home party that night. Captain Gates and another man, a Mr. Stroud by name, had come to stay for a few days' shooting, and they certainly proved lively additions to our gathering. In the midst of a buzz of conversation and laughter, there was, as so often happens, a sudden lull, and then Kenneth from the other side of the table suddenly broke the silence:

'Miss Thorn, Nell here wants to know the name of the book

you were studying so deeply this afternoon in the corn-field?'

My cheeks flushed a little; for one moment I hesitated, and every one seemed to be waiting for my answer; then I said in a tolerably steady voice,

'It was my Bible.'

I felt, rather than saw, the astonishment depicted on the faces of those at the table.

Nelly, who was always overflowing with fun, burst out laughing:

'You don't mean to say that you are religious?' she said; but her mother hushed her rather sharply, and changed the subject at once.

I felt I had difficult times coming. Later on in the evening, when music was going on, Captain Gates came over to me as I sat looking out into the dusky garden by one of the long French windows, and said,

'I see you have no difficulty in showing your colours, Miss Thorn.'

I looked up at him gravely. 'I ought to have no difficulty,' I said; 'it is nothing to be ashamed of.'

He smiled, and leaning against the half-open window seemed to regard me with some amusement.

'Is it a rude question to ask with whom you have been living before you came here?'

I told him, and then he said reflectively,

'It's a strange thing why the Bible should be thought so out of place sometimes; but I wonder now if you read it out of pure pleasure, or only from a sense of duty?'

'Why, I love it!' I exclaimed; then a little impulsively I added,

'I don't mind telling you, Captain Gates, or any one else, for that matter, it is only just lately that I have felt so differently about it. I used to think it dull and tedious, but it has changed now, or rather, I have changed, and there is nothing I like better than getting away alone somewhere and having a nice read all by myself.'

'You will not find much quiet time in this house,' he rejoined. 'We are always on the go here; you have come into a different life. I fancy your Bible reading will soon be a thing of the past.'

'Never, I hope!' I said a little warmly. 'I don't mean to lead a gay life, Captain Gates; I don't care for those kind of things now!'

He laughed. 'Perhaps you have never tried it?'

'I never mean to.'

Our conversation was interrupted here, and for the rest of the evening I said very little to any one; but a short time after I had been in my bedroom that night Nelly, knocked at my door.

'I'm coming in for a talk,' she said; 'I'm very curious about you. Do you know that we have all been discussing you downstairs?'

Amy Le Feuvre

'I dare say,' I said, laughing. Somehow, I felt very much drawn to Nelly; she seemed such a pleasant, outspoken girl. Constance, the eldest of them, though full of life and spirits, was rather cold and distant in manner towards me. In fact, she had given me the impression that my arrival had not been welcome to her.

Nelly seated herself in a low rocking-chair, and scanned me rather mischievously before she proceeded:

'You are such a pretty, bright little thing to look at, that Bible reading seems so incongruous! Of course, I read my Bible in the evening when I go to bed—at least, when I am not too tired—but that's a different matter. Mother said we mustn't take any notice of you, and you would soon shake off these notions; but Captain Gates said you told him you didn't intend to lead a gay life as we do—you have evidently taken him into your confidence—and he said he would back you against us for your determination of purpose. Now will you take my advice, Hilda? Don't look so hot and uncomfortable. You haven't come into a houseful of saints, you know, so you can't expect us to fall in with your views at once. Mother, of course, won't like it if you go against her plans for you; she will be very vexed, but she will eventually give in; but it's a different matter with father, and he is your guardian, remember. He hates "cant," as he calls it, and he has great ideas of your taking your position in society as you should. If you cross his will, I warn you you will bring the house down upon your ears; he never will stand any opposition. And what father will do by his authority, Kenneth will do out of sheer love of teasing. He will lead you a life of it, I can tell you; so I warn you beforehand.'

'But,' I said, flushing a little, though I tried to speak quietly, 'I have no intention of setting up my will in opposition to your father's—I wouldn't dream of it. What do you think me like, Nelly?'

Nelly laughed. 'I think you are a curiosity,' she said, 'and whether we shall crush your originality out of you in a few weeks' time, remains to be proved. I thought I would give you a friendly intimation of what to expect. And now good-night!'

She left me, and, perplexed and troubled by her words, I went to my window, and, opening the casement, leant out to cool my hot cheeks. Such a soft, still night it was! As I raised my eyes to the innumerable stars above, and felt the hush and solemnity of the darkness, again the words came to me: 'Dwell deep.' What did it matter if I found I should have a cross to take up, if I had to bear a little teasing from others who did not think as I did? When I realized in the depths of my heart the riches I had, and the stores of hidden wealth of which they knew nothing, I could rest down upon it with such comfort, feeling that my inner life would be sustained and strengthened by One who never left me. And so I went to sleep that night at perfect peace in my new surroundings.

Amy Le Feuvre

CHAPTER II

TAKING A STAND

'Who is not afraid to say his say,
Though a whole town's against him.'

—Longfellow

I was soon at home with the Forsyths. Nelly and Violet treated me as a sister, and Constance was too much engrossed at present with her own concerns to take much notice of me. Kenneth was the only one who was continually bringing forward serious topics of conversation in my presence, and requesting me to give him my views on them. He never let me alone, and though I tried to keep out of his way, and say as little as possible, I found it increasingly difficult. Captain Gates more than once came to my rescue; but since I felt he had betrayed my confidence a few evenings before, I could not talk with the same freedom to him.

I saw very little of General Forsyth. He spent the greater part of his time out of doors, and it was only in the evening that he joined us all. His children, though fond of him, never seemed to feel at ease in his company, and I soon found that his will was law with all.

One afternoon soon after my arrival I went out for a stroll across the fields at the back of the house. I felt I wanted to be alone, and away from the constant chatter and laughter of the girls. So I wandered on farther than I had intended, and found myself at last on the edge of a wild moor. My thoughts were grave ones, but very happy ones; and as I gazed over the broad expanse of heather in front of me away into the blue distance, where the soft fleecy clouds seemed to stoop and kiss the outlines of purple hills as they swept gently by, I could not help thanking God with all my heart that He had brought me into my present surroundings.

Suddenly I was startled by hearing close to me a child's sobs, and after some minutes' search I came upon a tiny boy crouched amongst the heather, grasping a bunch of faded harebells in his chubby fist, and crying as if his heart would break.

As I bent over him, he looked up into my face and sobbed out pitifully,—

'Cally me home, lady; I wants my mother.'

'You poor little mite!' I said. 'What is your name? and where do you live?'

But as I lifted him up he uttered a sharp cry. 'My foots is hurted; I tumbled down, and I've losted my boot.'

I saw that this was indeed the case; his little foot was cut and bleeding, perhaps from coming in contact with some sharp stone, and I was for a moment at a loss what to do. He seemed about three or four years old, but a heavily built child, and my heart sank at the prospect of carrying him. Yet this was the only alternative, and as he seemed to have very little idea of where he lived, I decided to bring him back with

　　　　　　　Amy Le Feuvre

me to our village, there being no other houses in sight.

He was quite willing to be carried, and wound his fat little arms so tightly round my neck that I thought he would throttle me. But my progress was painfully slow; the sun blazed down with fierceness, and there was no shade on the moor; even the fresh breeze which I had so enjoyed in coming seemed to have disappeared, and every now and then I had to stop and rest. The child himself soon dropped asleep in my arms, and I became so tired myself that I was strongly inclined to leave him lying on the heather, and send some one to fetch him when I got home. At last, to my great relief, as I was crossing a field I saw a figure approaching, and this proved to be Kenneth.

'Halloo!' he said, when he caught sight of me and my burden, 'what on earth have you got here? You are certainly the most extraordinary young person that we have had in these parts for a long time! Where have you picked up this small fry? Are you taking a pilgrimage and doing penance for your sins with him? If you only could see your face! It makes me burn to look at you!'

'Don't tease,' I said wearily, as I tried in vain to disengage the little fellow's arms from round my neck. 'I found him crying amongst the heather, and he has hurt his foot and cannot walk. Do take him from me, will you?'

This was not such an easy matter. The child woke up cross, screamed when Kenneth took him, and with his little fist struck him full in the face with all his childish strength, crying out,—

'I won't be callied by you; I wants the lady.'

Kenneth tossed him across his shoulder with calm

indifference to his cries.

'I shall have a reckoning with you by-and-by, young man, for this assault. He is the infant pickle of our village, Miss Thorn —commonly called Roddy Walters; his mother keeps the small general shop, and Roddy keeps her pretty lively with his pranks. His last mania has been running away whenever he gets a chance, and if you intend to carry him home from wherever you find him, you will have enough to do, I can tell you.'

I made no reply, for I felt quite exhausted, and was greatly relieved to find that Kenneth knew where to take him.

Presently I was asked,—

'Been having a Bible study on the moor this afternoon?'

'No,' I said quietly, 'I have not.'

'That's a pity, isn't it? You have been out all the afternoon; it's rather frivolous, isn't it, and a waste of precious time to be sauntering over the moor doing nothing? A time of meditation, perhaps?'

Yes,' I answered, smiling a little in spite of myself, 'I have been thinking, as I walked, what lovely country it is round here.'

'We are going to have some grand doings in our neighbourhood soon,' Kenneth pursued after a few moments' silence; 'the autumn manoeuvres are coming on, and every one round here keeps open house. We generally start the ball rolling by a dance. Are you fond of dancing?'

'I used to be fond of it at school,' I said, 'but I—I don't care about it now.'

I felt he was trying to draw me out, and resolved to say as little as possible.

'Ah! you wait till you're in the thick of it, and see the scarlet jackets flying round. All the girls here lose their heads, and their hearts, too, for the matter of that. I was telling that fellow Stroud to-day that if he means anything, he had better cut in at once and get it settled, for Constance will have nothing to say to him a few weeks later.'

I said nothing; I had noticed Mr. Stroud's attentions to Constance, and had drawn my own conclusions; but when Kenneth went on in the same strain declaring that Constance would keep him hanging on till she saw any she liked better, I turned upon him rather sharply,—

'I am very thankful you are not my brother. I think it is a shame of you to talk so, and I won't listen to any more of it!'

He laughed, and as we were now entering the village there was little more conversation between us till we had reached the small general shop. Mrs. Walters came out to us in a great state of excitement, and Roddy, who had nearly fallen asleep again, woke up and began to cry at the top of his voice.

'I'm sure I don't know what to do with him,' she complained; 'he runs away from school whenever he get a chance, and last Sunday he breaks into my neighbour's chicken-house, and smashes a whole set of eggs that was being 'atched! School do keep him a bit quiet in the week, but Sundays he's just rampageous!'

'Does he go to Sunday School?' I asked.

'There's no Sunday School in our village, miss; the bigger ones they goes to the next parish; but it's two good miles, and my Roddy he can't walk so fur. Now thank the leddy and gentleman, you scamp, for bringin' you home!'

Roddy turned his big blue eyes upon us, then suddenly held out his arms to me.

'I'll kiss her, for she callied me much nicer nor the gempleum!'

I gave the little fellow a hug. He looked such a baby in his mother's arms, and I felt quite drawn to him.

'I love little children so,' I said to Kenneth as we were walking home. 'I wish there was a Sunday School in this place. I should like Roddy in my class.'

'You might start a Sunday School,' suggested Kenneth gravely. 'Our old rector will let you do exactly as you like, I am sure.'

'I wonder if I could,' I said reflectively; 'just a class for the little ones, and those that can't walk as far as the bigger, stronger ones. I should be glad if I could do something on Sunday.'

Then remembering to whom I was speaking, I checked myself and said no more on the subject, though my thoughts were busy.

When we came up to the house we found that afternoon tea was going on under the old elms on the lawn. Mrs. Forsyth was in a low wicker-chair with her work, Constance was pouring out tea, and Nelly was swinging lazily in a hammock, whilst Captain Gates and Mr. Stroud were making themselves generally agreeable.

'Have you two been taking a walk together?' asked Nelly as we approached. 'I have been hunting for you everywhere, Hilda. Lady Walker has been calling, and wanted to see you; she used to know your mother.'

'How warm you look!' observed Constance, eyeing me, I felt, with disapproval. 'What have you been doing?'

I sat down on the garden seat, glad to rest, and Kenneth, leaning against the tree opposite, began:—

'Well now, I will give you a true account of her. She felt so disgusted with our frivolity at lunch, that she went out to get away from us; she wandered on dreaming her dreams and building her castles in the air, mourning over our depravity, and lamenting that she had no scope with us for all her benevolent projects, until she found herself out upon the moor, whereupon she looked round, and after a time found Roddy Walters asleep. It was an opportunity to act the Good Samaritan; she hoisted him up into her arms in spite of his howls, and insisted upon carrying him home. And I met her panting and struggling with him in old Drake's meadows.'

'But why didn't you let him walk, Hilda?' interrupted Nelly.

'He had hurt his foot, poor little fellow—it was impossible; even your brother saw that, for he carried him the rest of the way himself.'

'And now,' pursued Kenneth gravely, 'the upshot is that she is so aghast at the state of heathenism and wickedness that the village children are in, that she is going to start a Sunday School herself next Sunday, and I expect she hopes to enlist some of us as teachers. Will you go, Gates? I will back you up.'

'Oh, I will go as a scholar,' said Captain Gates readily.

'I think, Kenneth, you are letting your tongue run on too fast,' said Mrs. Forsyth gently; 'I am quite sure Hilda has no such intentions.'

I felt myself getting vexed under all this chaffing, but it has always been my way to speak out, and so, turning to Mrs. Forsyth, I said,—

'He is not representing it fairly, Mrs. Forsyth. Mrs. Walters was telling us she wished she could send Roddy to Sunday School, and I said how much I wished I could have him to teach. It was Mr. Kenneth who suggested my having a Sunday School. I certainly liked the idea, and meant to speak to you about it, but not now.'

Kenneth laughed. 'You meant to have a private confabulation with the mater and the parson, but we like everything above board here. We haven't much to amuse us, and so every one likes to know every one else's business. I can see you have an eye for reform, so think it just as well to warn others about you.'

'Hilda,' said Mrs. Forsyth, who evidently wished to change the subject, 'Lady Walker has invited you to go to some theatricals next Wednesday with the girls. I told her you had no engagement; you will enjoy it, I hope. They live a little distance off in a beautiful old abbey, and are very nice people.'

There was silence; I felt that difficulties were all round me this afternoon, and perhaps being so tired helped to make me less willing to assert my views. I sipped my cup of tea before replying, and then said quietly,—

'It was very kind of her to ask me.'

'It will be great fun, Hilda. The Walkers are awfully good at that kind of thing, and they are going to have the stage out of doors. I wish I was going to take part in it, but we shall finish up with a dance after, so I shall keep myself for that.'

Silently I put up a prayer for courage, and then replied,—

'I don't think I shall go, Nelly; I do not care about theatricals nor dancing.'

'I have accepted for you,' said Mrs. Forsyth quickly and decidedly, 'for General Forsyth wishes you to go. I am afraid you must keep your likes and dislikes in the background whilst with us about matters like this.' And taking up her work she left us and went towards the house, whilst I felt my cheeks burn, as I realized how displeased she was at my speech.

Nelly began laughing and talking with Captain Gates, Constance and Mr. Stroud soon strolled away, and I sat on, conscious that Kenneth's eyes were upon me, yet feeling so uncertain of myself that I dared not speak. I think I was very near tears. Presently Nelly turned to me: 'Have you finished your tea, Hilda? will you come and get some flowers for the dinner-table?'

I jumped up, tired though I was, and when we were out of hearing of the others, Nelly put her hand caressingly on my arm:—

'You poor little thing, you have been having a hot time of it since you came back from your walk. I feel awfully sorry for you. Mother is vexed, of course, but she will have forgotten all about it by the time she next sees you. She is never angry for long. Captain Gates said to me just now that you were not wanting in courage or straightforwardness; you spoke up well, Hilda; but I have warned you beforehand, you had much better, as mother says, keep your likes and dislikes to yourself. As Captain Gates was saying, if a person feels in a foreign element, the only cure is to adapt themselves to it. He is taking quite an interest in you, Hilda; he told me you had a true ring about you. But it is awfully funny to me, your standing out against all innocent pleasure.'

'I will talk to you about it another day, Nelly,' I said, trying to speak gently; 'don't think me disobliging if I leave you now. I am so tired that I feel I cannot walk another step. You don't mind getting the flowers by yourself, do you?'

'Of course I don't. Go up to your room and have a nap; you will have a quiet time till dinner.'

I left her, for I felt I must be alone; and when I reached my room I took my Bible, and sitting down in the low window seat turned over its leaves for comfort and guidance. My thoughts were perplexed ones. How I longed to live at peace with every one! How easy it would be to slip along in this pleasant family life, doing as others did around me; how increasingly difficult I should find it, if I was continually setting myself up in opposition to all their plans and wishes for me! And yet in my heart I knew that unless I took a stand from the first, I should be drawn into a whirl of gaiety, such as I felt would not be the right position for a true Christian to be found in. Then I wondered what claims my guardian had upon me, how far it would be right to obey him, and where I must draw the line. 'If only I had some one to advise me!' I murmured, and the next minute felt ashamed of the thought as these words met my eye,—

Amy Le Feuvre

'But the Comforter, which is the Holy Ghost, whom the Father will send in My name, He shall teach you all things.'

I bowed my head in prayer, and when a little later I turned again to my Bible I was not long left in doubt. 'Be not conformed to this world,' I read in Romans. I turned up the references: 'Not fashioning yourselves according to the former lusts in your ignorance.' 'Love not the world, neither the things that are in the world.' 'Wherefore come out from among them, and be ye separate, saith the Lord.' As I sat there drinking in these messages, and dwelling upon them each in turn, all doubt and hesitation left me. I was quieted and refreshed, and when the thought of my guardian's possible anger flitted across my mind, I was able to put it aside—'He shall teach you all things.'

And that took me to another verse, 'Take ye no thought how or what thing ye shall answer, or what ye shall say; for the Holy Ghost shall teach you in the same hour what ye ought to say.'

With this I was quite content.

CHAPTER III

THE REASON WHY

Let us, then, be what we are, and speak what we think,
and in all things
Keep ourselves loyal to truth.'

—*Longfellow*

'General Forsyth, may I speak to you for a few minutes?'

It was after breakfast the next morning that I made this
request. I was determined to have the matter settled as soon
as possible.

'Certainly,' my guardian said, looking at me in some surprise.
'Come into the library, for we shall be undisturbed there.'

He led the way, politely handed me a chair, and then stood
leaning his back against the mantel-piece and stroking his
moustache, giving me at the same time a keen glance from
under his shaggy eyebrows.

'Well,' he said, 'what is it? Do you want any money?'

'No,' I said a little nervously; 'it is quite another matter;' then

Amy Le Feuvre

gathering courage, I looked him straight in the face and said, 'General Forsyth, I think you expect me to go to those theatricals at the Walkers' next week. I cannot do it.'

'Indeed!' he said lightly, 'is it a question of dress? What is the difficulty?'

'No, it is not that. I want to tell you now, for I think it may save difficulties afterwards. I do not wish to lead a gay life: I cannot go to dances or theatres with an easy conscience. Don't think it a mere whim or passing fancy; it is a matter of principle with me. I have given myself to God for His service, and I look at everything in that light, and from that standpoint.'

General Forsyth looked amused.

'Don't put so much tragedy in your tone, child! Since when have you taken up these peculiar notions?'

'About two or three months ago,' I replied. 'It has made a great difference in my life. I thought if I explained my reason to you, you would not press me to go to things which are thoroughly distasteful to me.'

'If it is only a couple of months since you formed these views, I think you will find that time will alter them, Hilda. I should like to state to you that, according to your father's will, I am to have full control of your money until you marry, or if that does not occur soon, until you are thirty years of age. After that you are your own mistress. Are you aware of this?'

'I did not quite understand it so,' I said, wondering at the turn our conversation was taking.

'I tell you this because it explains our position towards each other. So much for the terms of the will. Now for what will touch you closer: I was with your father when he died in India; he was one of my dearest friends, as you know, and on his dying bed he made me promise that when your education was finished I should look after you as one of my own daughters, see that you were given every advantage due to the position in society that he meant you to occupy, and in fact be to you what he would have been had he lived. I know what his views were for you, and those views I shall conscientiously try to further whilst you are with me. I shall not countenance for a moment your hiding away from friends of your parents, and others with whom I wish you to associate. A time will come when you will thank me for my firmness now, and for refusing to allow you to sacrifice all your prospects in life to some morbid fancies that you must have picked up in some Dissenting chapel.'

I was silent for a moment, then I said,—

'I think my father would have wished me to be happy, General Forsyth; I cannot go against my conscience in this matter, it would make me wretched. I do feel very grateful to you for giving me a home; but indeed I would rather go away and earn my own living than lead the life you have planned out for me.'

'We will not discuss the matter further,' said General Forsyth icily; 'I have told you my wishes on the subject. If I am to treat you as one of my own daughters, you will accompany them wherever they go. I am accustomed to be obeyed in my own house, and I do not think you will deliberately oppose my wishes for you.'

'I am sorry to displease you,' I said in a low voice, 'but in this one respect I feel I am right in acting so'; and then I left the room with a heavy heart. I went out into the garden a little later, and made my way to a quiet spot in a plantation near the house, where I had found a delightful little nook to sit in, and there I took my Bible and had a quiet read and prayer. General Forsyth was not in to luncheon, but I saw from Mrs. Forsyth's face that he had told her of our interview. She said very little to me, and when the theatricals were mentioned at the table she changed the subject at once.

In the afternoon I joined Violet and her governess in an expedition to a wood a little distance off. We took tea with us, and I thoroughly enjoyed it. Miss Graham was a quiet woman, but very clever, and she and her pupil were the best of friends.

'I wish you were in the schoolroom with me,' said Violet, as we sat chatting together in the cool shade under the trees. 'I think we should have great fun together, and do you know, I heard mother say to Constance this morning that she wished you were too, for then the difficulty would be solved. What did she mean?'

I gave an involuntary sigh, and Miss Graham looked at me a little curiously; then, as Violet started to her feet in pursuit of a squirrel, she laid her hand gently on my arm.

'You look troubled, Miss Thorn; I am afraid you are one of those who try to go through life too seriously, isn't it so?'

'I don't think so,' I said with a smile; 'I am a little troubled to-day because I am vexing both General and Mrs. Forsyth very much, I am afraid, but I cannot help it.'

'Ah! don't do it, my dear. Take their advice, and trust them about your life here. They are old, and you are young. I have heard from Nelly a little about your difficulty, and I am sorry for you, for I admire your sincerity. Still, we see things differently when we get older, and you will find that it is always best to give way to others, and keep your own opinions in the background, especially when you are young.'

'It isn't my opinions that I want to bring forward,' I said, 'but I am old enough to be responsible for my actions.'

'There was a time when I had such thoughts,' said Miss Graham; 'when I was quite a young girl I used to long to join a Sisterhood, and devote myself to good works for the rest of my life; but I was shown how visionary and unpractical such ideas were, and after a time I ceased to entertain them.'

'Why did you want to give yourself up to good works, Miss Graham?' I asked a little curiously.

She laughed. 'Well, if you really want to know, it was partly because I had met with a disappointment. Some one I was very fond of—in fact, to whom I was engaged, left me to marry a girl with money, and I was for the time disgusted with life. Then I think I did desire to live a useful life; but now I have realized there are many different ways of doing that.'

'I don't wonder you changed your mind, if those were your motives for leaving the world,' I said slowly.

'Why, what other motives would you have? What is yours? Isn't it a desire to be good and fit yourself for heaven one day?'

'No,' I replied softly; 'it isn't to earn my salvation that I want to keep clear of the world; it is because I have had that given to me already, and I want to show my love to the Saviour by my life. I do love Him, and I am so afraid of a whirl of gaiety spoiling the communion I have with Him day by day.'

Miss Graham looked at me in astonishment, and was about to speak, when Violet came back, and we changed the conversation. I do not know how it was that I spoke so openly to Miss Graham, for I generally found it very difficult to express my thoughts to any one; but I seemed to have been led into it, and as we walked back in the cool of the evening I just put up a prayer that she might be made to see things differently.

I was rather relieved to hear that General and Mrs. Forsyth were dining out that night. Perhaps their absence accounted for the extra gaiety of our party; I had never seen Constance and Nelly so full of spirits, and Kenneth and Captain Gates seemed bent upon having 'a real good time of it,' as they expressed it. Hugh kept them a little in check at dinner; but when they joined us in the drawing-room afterwards, I saw they meant to be as good as their word.

Constance sat down to the piano and began playing some waltzes, and then Captain Gates sprang up. 'Here, Kenneth, give me a hand; we will move some of these obstacles, and have a dance.'

In a few minutes, chairs had been piled up one on top of the other in a corner, tables and couches pushed to the side, and a clear space left in the middle of the room.

Hugh made his exit in disgust, saying, 'I think it is a romp, not a dance, that you are wanting!'

And Mr. Stroud, a quiet little man, said protestingly, 'I think you will find it very warm work in here; would you not rather take a stroll by the river, Miss Forsyth?'

Constance shook her head, and continued playing, and then, before I knew where I was, Nelly seized hold of me and, whirling me round, waltzed away. I could not help enjoying it; I had always loved dancing at school, so without a thought I gave myself up to it; and when Captain Gates stopped us, declaring that he would not waltz with Kenneth, and we must make a speedy exchange, I made no objection. I danced with him and with Kenneth afterwards, and then took Constance's place at the piano, to let her have a turn.

When we were all tired out and were resting Kenneth said,—

'I think we are in good form for the Walkers' wind-up now. What do you think, Miss Thorn? You have changed your mind about going, haven't you?'

'No,' I said decidedly, 'I am not going.'

'Nonsense!' Nelly exclaimed, 'you are. Mother said this morning that it was settled, and why on earth do you want to keep away? you dance like—'

'Like a midsummer elf,' put in Captain Gates; 'I thought you did not care about dancing. Why, you love it, you know you do!'

I felt my cheeks flush, as I realized how foolish I had been, and then I said, resolving to be truthful at all events,—

'Well, I thought I did not care for it. I did not know till Nelly started me off how enjoyable it is still to me. But that does not alter my decision at all about going to the theatricals next Wednesday.'

'It is those, then, that you dislike, not the dancing?'

Amy Le Feuvre

I did not answer. Kenneth now spoke from the depth of a large couch upon which he had thrown himself.

'Now look here, Goody Two-Shoes, just stand up and give us a discourse on the iniquities of dancing and such like. Here is your opportunity; five worldlings before you! Shall I ring the bell for Tomkins to fetch your Bible? I would go myself, only I'm just about done up. You will want a text. Give us your views; it will be most interesting and edifying. Who knows? You may so convince us of the awful sin of going to the Walkers', that we shall all send in an apology for our absence, and from henceforth do our dancing at home!'

'Joking apart, we should really like to know your reasons for abstaining from evening parties,' said Captain Gates.

Still I was silent, feeling the difficulty of my position; and then, after a swift prayer for guidance, I said slowly: 'I don't think any of you will understand me, and I am very sorry I have been carried away to-night by the music. It isn't dancing itself that's a sin, and I am not judging any of you; but I know in my heart that dancing and theatricals are wrong for me; they are the essentials of worldliness, those and horse-racing, and card-playing, and other things of the same sort. I want to keep clear of them all, as I know if I go in for any I shall be gradually more and more engrossed in them. And the very proof I have had to-night of how my taste for dancing has not gone, will make me keep right away from it for the future.'

'But why is it such a sin for you?' asked Nelly wonderingly.

'Because,' I said, feeling the colour rise to my cheeks with the effort of speaking out,—'because I have given myself, body and soul, to God, and I want to live only for Him. You asked me for a text—here is the one that has helped me: "He died for all, that they which live should not henceforth live unto themselves, but unto Him which died for them and rose again."'

There was silence, then Constance said with a light laugh: 'To be consistent, Hilda, you ought to go into a Sisterhood; are you thinking of doing it?'

'No; why should I? I only tell you this to show you how inconsistent I should be if I threw myself into the midst of a gay life and thought of nothing but enjoying myself.'

'Like the rest of us? Give me one of your sort for parading their own virtues at the expense of their neighbours!' said Kenneth, with a yawn.

'Oh, please don't say that! You made me give my reasons.'

'And so you have drawn out this hard-and-fast line of life for yourself, and think you will be happy in stifling all your natural instincts?' asked Captain Gates.

'I am happy—I don't want these things I have something much better!' Then, warming with my subject, I added impulsively, 'I don't believe any of you know what it is to realize that religion is not an outward form, something we hear and read about, but is a reality in one's soul. It is living instead of merely existing, it is being in touch with every-thing beautiful and ennobling, and with a living personal Friend, whose love is such an utterly different thing from anything else on earth!'

'I think we have had enough,' Kenneth interrupted in a draw-ling tone. 'Spare us any more rhapsodies. Can't we have a little music? You might give us a song, Stroud.'

Mr. Stroud complied with this request at once; he seemed never so happy as when Constance was playing his accompanyments, and for the next twenty minutes she and he were singing together. Then Captain Gates asked me a little hesitatingly if I would play on my violin. I had not often used it since I had been with the Forsyths, but I had always been very fond of it, and had played for hours to my old cousin in London.

'I think a violin is rather worldly,' objected Kenneth in his mocking tone; 'I am sure it is not a fit conclusion to the sermon we have just been hearing.'

'I don't think it is at all worldly,' I said determinedly, as I moved across to one of the long French windows and took my violin from the case; then leaning against the side of the window I looked out into the soft summer night, and dreamily began to play.

Perhaps it was the absence of General and Mrs. Forsyth that made me feel more at ease, but instead of playing any of my classical pieces I drifted into improvising as I went along, and then, as my thoughts took me far away, I gave myself up to them entirely. 'Dwell deep' was ringing softly but clearly in my ears. Storms could come and storms could go, but in all and through all were those two little words of peace and quiet. And my violin was with me, and understood my mood. I don't know how long I played, but when I came to myself and surroundings, soothed and comforted in spirit, I found them all staring at me in astonishment. I let my bow fall in perfect silence, and Captain Gates asked with a long-drawn breath, 'What is the name of that?'

'Dwell deep!' I replied with a full heart; and then putting my violin by, without another word I left them, and went up to my room. I did not go down again that night.

CHAPTER IV

AN OPENING FOR WORK

'Whoever fears God, fears to sit at ease.'

—E. B. Browning

'Hilda, mother wants to speak to you in her boudoir. We have just been having a grand discussion about our dresses for the Walkers' affair, and she wants to find out from you whether you are really going or not.'

I sighed as Nelly finished speaking.

I was picking some roses on the lawn, and Captain Gates had just sauntered out of the smoking-room, cigar in mouth.

It was such a lovely morning that I was meditating spending it in my favourite nook in the plantation, and for the time I had forgotten everything unpleasant.

'You poor little creature!' said Nelly sympathetically, 'aren't you tired of it? You have discussed the subject with father, given us a long preach last night, and now there still remains mother! Let me advise you, don't be too outspoken with her. Constance told her about our dance last night, and mother

Amy Le Feuvre

seems to think that it must be pure wilfulness on your part if you still refuse to go with us.'

'I wish I could be left alone,' I said a little wistfully; 'I shall only make your mother angry.'

'Are you tired of showing your colours?' questioned Captain Gates.

'I hope not,' I said in a brighter tone, and then I went into the house.

Mrs. Forsyth was kind at first, but when she saw that I was really determined she became vexed.

'It is placing me in a very awkward position, Hilda. What excuse can I make for you? You have not even delicacy of health to account for your absence. I am anxious to take you about with my own daughters, and people will think I am purposely keeping you in the background. I do wish you had given us some intimation of these strange views before you came to live with us. It will be a continual annoyance to us.'

'Do you think I had better go back to my cousin's in London?' I asked. 'I really do not want to be such a trouble. If you would only let me be happy in my own way, and stay quietly at home, I should be so grateful, because you have all been so kind to me that I love to be here.'

'I really don't know what we shall do with you,' Mrs. Forsyth replied, in a milder tone. 'I believe General Forsyth has his own plans for you, and if you will not fall in with them, it would be better for us all that you should be away from us. However, of course, we cannot force you to go with us next Wednesday, so I must try and explain it as best I can to Lady Walker. I need hardly say that General Forsyth will not be at all pleased about it.'

I left her feeling rather downhearted. Looking at it from their point of view, I must be somewhat of a trial to them, and yet I knew I could not act otherwise.

As I was stepping out into the garden again, deep in thought, I was startled by the sudden appearance of little Roddy Walters from behind a large tree close to the house. His hands were full of yellow marsh marigolds and blue forget-me-nots.

'Roddy has brought them for you,' were his first words, as he caught sight of me.

I had seen the little fellow several times since our first meeting, but this was the first time that he had ventured to come up to the house to see me, though whenever I passed through the village he would run after me, and I had great difficulty in getting away from him.

'How lovely!' I exclaimed, as I took the bunch from his hot little hands; 'but, Roddy, you ought to be at school. Have you run away?'

He laughed and nodded: 'Bess Brown did take me to school, but she slapped me, and I runned away, and Jim tooked me down to the water, and we picked these booful flowers, and I loves you, and Jim said I might give 'em to you.'

'And who is Jim?'

'Jim is waiting for me, Jim is, he's sittin' on the gate; you come and I'll show you him.'

He led me down the avenue as fast as his little legs could

Amy Le Feuvre

carry him, and there on a side gate that led into some fields was a lad about fifteen. He got down directly he saw me, and I noticed that he was a cripple and had a crutch by his side.

'Are you Jim?' I asked.

'Yes, mum!'

'Don't you know that Roddy ought to be at school? It isn't right of you to encourage him to play truant.'

Jim laughed. 'He's such a little 'un, he is.'

And then we drifted into talk. Jim told me he lived with his uncle, who was a cobbler, but he himself had no occupation except that of gathering wild flowers, and taking them into the market town near, twice a week. I found to my surprise that he could not read.

'I was on my back for years when I might 'a had my school-in', and when I was able to get about with my crutch I was that 'shamed to go, being such a big 'un, and such a dunce. Uncle Sam, he has a tried to teach me, but he has a awful temper, and says I'm that slow I aggrewate him into fits.'

'How I wish I could teach you!' I exclaimed; 'wouldn't you like to learn?'

'Ay, shouldn't I! but I'm an awful dullard.'

We talked a little longer. I took a great fancy to this thin lanky lad, with his great dark questioning eyes—he seemed lonely—and his affection for little Roddy was very touching. That afternoon the old rector happened to call while we were at tea, and I took the opportunity of asking him about the boy; he seemed quite pleased at my interest in him, and then of his own accord he broached the subject of Sunday School.

'I should like to get one of you young ladies to have a class of the little ones on Sunday. I am an old man myself, and don't feel up to it. I sometimes wish I had a wife or daughter to help me about these things. Mrs. Forsyth, what do you think about it?'

'I have no doubt Miss Thorn would be delighted to do what you wish. She has already expressed a desire, I believe, to do something of the sort.'

Mrs. Forsyth's tone was a little stiff, but I was so glad that she made no objection to the suggestion that I felt quite grateful to her. And before the rector left us he had settled that I should start a class the following Sunday afternoon from three to four in the vestry of the little church.

'I will go round to my parishioners and let them know. Of course you will be prepared for very little ones, as the bigger ones attend a school a little distance off. And as for Jim Carter, if you can give him a reading lesson now and then in the week, I shall be delighted.'

When the rector had gone, I ran up to my room, and just knelt down and thanked God for the work He had already given me. Only that morning I had been praying for something to do, and had anticipated great difficulties in the way.

Yet the opening had come, and everything seemed made easy for me. And for the rest of the day this fresh interest made me forget my troubles, until I was reminded of them in the drawing-room that evening.

We were all there, General Forsyth reading the evening

paper, Mrs. Forsyth with her work, and the girls round the piano, when suddenly Kenneth said, turning to me,—

'What kind of a mood are you in to-night? A musical one? Because if so, please favour us with a repetition of last night's performance.'

'What? Another dance?' said Nelly laughing. 'She is never going to dance again, she says!'

'Wait and see,' and Kenneth's tone was a little scornful; 'but it was the violin I was alluding to.'

Then General Forsyth looked up.

'I hope you have thought better about going to Lady Walker's, Hilda. I hear you were nothing loth to turn this room into chaos last night in order to enjoy a dance, so I conclude you have overcome your foolish scruples about it.'

'I am sorry, General Forsyth,' I said, trying to speak bravely, 'but I told Mrs. Forsyth this morning that I cannot go.'

'You have your father's obstinacy, I see;' and throwing down his paper angrily, General Forsyth got up and left the room.

'Never saw the general lose his temper before,' murmured Mr. Stroud to Constance; and she replied, in tones loud enough for me to hear, 'She is a provoking little thing; I believe it is nothing but cant with her. I hate those kind of people.'

Captain Gates was sitting close to me, and his eyes met mine as we caught the sneering words. He did not say anything, but got up from his seat and fetched my violin, which he put into my hands saying,—

'Give us another treat, for you make it speak!'

I shook my head, then, as he begged me so hard, I felt I ought not to refuse, but I could not play as I had done the night before, and when I had finished he said,—

'Thank you, but that is rather different to last night.'

'It is rather too classical, perhaps. I will try a little lullaby. It's German, and I think you may like it.'

'Hilda,' said Mrs. Forsyth when I had finished, 'you ought to cultivate your gift for music, for you have got a good touch. I am anxious for Violet to play well, but her violin lessons with Miss Graham are a source of constant trouble to me. I wish you could give her a few hints about it. Miss Graham is a good musician, but she certainly does not handle the instrument as you do.'

'I shall be very glad to practise with Violet a little,' I said, 'if Miss Graham does not object.'

Then Nelly called to me from the balcony outside the windows, and I joined her with a sense of relief at getting out into the still, cool evening air.

Captain Gates joined us, and leant against one of the stone pillars enjoying a cigar.

We talked and laughed for some time, then as Nelly moved off a little farther to speak to Hugh, who had also come out, Captain Gates turned to me and said, 'You are having rather a hot time of it just now, Miss Thorn, I feel afraid. Why are you so determined in your views? I feel sorry for you, because you have every one against you.'

His tone was sympathetic.

'I shall get accustomed to that, I suppose,' I said; but as I looked away to the still hills in the distance, my eyes suddenly filled with tears, and I realized how lonely my position was.

'I can't think why you hold out; you are planning a dreary life for yourself, don't you think so?'

'No,' I said, hastily brushing away my tears, and smiling at his gloomy tone; 'I shall not be a bit dreary; how could I be!'

'I wish you would explain a few things to me, and then perhaps I should understand better. Do you consider us all dreadful sinners here?'

'I judge no one, Captain Gates. It seems to me you must have something to fill your life and interest and occupy you, and if you haven't got what I have, you must have worldly amusements.'

'And what have you got that we have not?'

I was silent for a moment, then I said,—

'Do you ever read your Bible, Captain Gates?'

'Not often.'

'You will find a great deal about the Christian's portion there, if you look; but I suppose the summing up of it all is just Christ Himself. If we have Him we want nothing more.'

There was another silence.

At length he said meditatively, 'I should like to be enlightened. Will you come for a row on the river to-morrow, and let us thrash the subject out?'

'I don't know,' I said hesitatingly; 'I will see what plans the others have.' And then I stepped back into the drawing-room, leaving him alone there, and wondering if he was really in earnest, or only drawing me out for his amusement.

When I went forward to wish General Forsyth 'good-night' that evening, he refused to take my hand, saying coldly, 'I shall have nothing to say to you for the present; your conduct is highly displeasing to me.'

I felt the blood rush to my cheeks, as he did not lower his voice, and all in the room heard his words; then I left the room slowly, like a naughty child being sent off to bed in disgrace. Nelly came rushing upstairs after me, and linked her arm in mine.

'Never mind, Hilda. You see father is never accustomed to have any one oppose him, and he cannot understand you. You are a bold little thing, to say what you do to him. Now tell me what conspiracy was going on between you and Captain Gates this evening? He is asking mother if we can have a picnic on the river to-morrow. Constance and Mr. Stroud are delighted, and mother has given her consent. Mother says she won't start with us, but may join us later in the day. He said we had better have three boats; but I wonder how we are going to pair off. I am not always going to be coupled with Kenneth, he and I are sure to fight. And I know Captain Gates will have you with him if he can manage it; he follows you about everywhere. Constance and Mr. Stroud are inseparable, and no one takes any notice of me!'

'Oh, Nelly, how you run on!' I exclaimed, half laughing, half vexed. 'I dare say I shall not go with you.'

'But you must; it will be great fun. Well, good night; I must be going.'

CHAPTER V

OPPORTUNITIES

'Draw through all failure to the perfect flower;
Draw through all darkness to the perfect light.
Yea, let the rapture of Thy spring-tide thrill
Through me, beyond me, till its ardour fill
The ungrowing souls that know not Thee aright,
That Thy great love may make of me, e'en me,
One added link to bind the world to Thee.'

—E. S. A.

We had a very enjoyable day up the river, Violet begged a holiday, and came with us. We had only two boats—Constance, Violet, and Mr. Stroud in one, and Nelly, Kenneth, Captain Gates, and I in the other. We took our lunch with us, and landed in a wood that came down to the water's edge. And after our meal was over Captain Gates asked me to come for a stroll through the woods with him. I did not feel inclined to do this at first, yet hardly liked to refuse, and it was not long before he turned our conversation towards serious subjects.

'I looked into a Bible which was in my room last night, Miss Thorn, but I couldn't see anything in it to make me wish to

Amy Le Feuvre

alter my life. It seems to me that as long as we slip along, and live decent, respectable lives, that is all that is required. God is merciful, isn't He? He won't require too much of us.'

'"What doth the Lord thy God require of thee, but to fear the Lord thy God, to walk in all His ways and to love Him, and to serve the Lord thy God with all thy heart and with all thy soul?"'

I repeated this verse rather slowly, adding,—

'I don't think many of us can say we come up to God's requirements, Captain Gates. "God will put up with a great many things in the human heart, but there is one thing He will not put up with in it—a second place." He who offers God a second place offers Him no place. I think that has been very truly said; don't you think so?'

'Well, I must plead guilty, of course, when you bring up a verse like that,' he responded lightly; 'but that is an impossible standard to set up for us poor human mortals.'

'Yes,' I said, after a minute's silence, 'judging us from that standard, we have all failed. We are "condemned already." I don't believe, Captain Gates, that we can ever be in real earnest about having our souls saved till we realize our condemnation. The verse that made me miserable was this one: "He that believeth not the Son shall not see life, but the wrath of God abideth on him."'

'Were you ever an unbeliever, then?' and Captain Gates looked at me curiously as he spoke.

'Of course I believed *about* Jesus Christ,' I replied in a low voice, 'but I didn't believe *in* Him. I hadn't come to Him and accepted my pardon at His hands. I didn't understand that, however good I might try to be, I could never expect to enter heaven unless I was washed and cleansed by Him.'

There was silence, and I was afraid I had been too out-spoken. Then, as we were passing a bush, with the most lovely honeysuckle at the top of it, I stopped and asked him if he would get me some.

This he willingly did, and as he handed me some beautiful sprays of it said,—

'There is no uncertain sound about your preaching, Miss Thorn. I believe you could do something with me if you were to try, but your doctrines are strange to me, and it will take me some time to get reconciled to them. You must take me in hand; will you?'

I looked up, and our eyes met. Again I wondered if he were sincere.

'I think you will find all you need in the Bible,' I said; and then I changed the conversation.

A few minutes after we met some of the others, and when we came down to the river's side Violet seized hold of my arm.

'Hilda, you come in our boat. I had an awfully dull time of it coming here. I think I was put in to act gooseberry, and I'm not going to do it again. Do come!'

'I will, of course, if Constance likes.'

And that was the order in which we came home, for Mrs. Forsyth never appeared at all. I was not surprised when Nelly came to me the last thing at night, as she was so fond of doing, and announced,—

Amy Le Feuvre

'Well, it is all settled. Constance and Mr. Stroud are engaged, and I wish her joy of him. Mother is pleased, because he has a nice little property; but I wouldn't have him for all the properties in creation. He is a regular stick, and hasn't a spark of fun in him. I only hope he won't stay on here after next week. Both he and Captain Gates said they must go when the Walkers' theatricals are over.'

'Is Constance very happy about it?' I asked.

'She seems to be, in her way. Of course, everything is rose colour to-night. Hilda, do you like Captain Gates?'

'Yes, I like him pretty well,' I said.

Nelly came up and put both hands on my shoulders.

'Now, look me straight in the face, and say that again.'

'I don't know what you mean,' I said, confronting her steadily.

'Sometimes I wonder if you are as innocent as you appear,' Nelly continued, laughing. 'But let me warn you of this: he is a great flirt, and tries it on with every girl he comes across. Kenneth asked him to-night downstairs if he thought a saint would make any man a good wife, and I never saw him so put out. He went off in a huff, and Kenneth said he thought he was hit at last. What did you talk about, Hilda, when you and he went off for your solitary ramble?'

I have always been told that I have an easy temper, but Nelly was never nearer making me really angry than she was that night.

'I wish you would not speak so, Nelly,' I said, flushing a little as I turned away from her; 'I cannot bear that kind of talk; as if you cannot be friendly to any one without having such motives ascribed to you. Captain Gates talks to me like any one else; he is a little more polite to me than your brothers are, that is the only difference.'

'My dear, how your eyes are flashing! I shall begin to be quite frightened of you. I didn't ascribe any motives to *you*, but I only warned you to beware of Captain Gates. He told Kenneth you were a bewitching little thing two days after he had first seen you, and I think the fact of your being so different to the usual run of girls he sees fascinates him for the time. I was going to advise you how to deal with him, but really I hardly dare now.'

'I don't mean to be cross, Nelly; but I am tired, and I want to be left alone.'

She laughed, gave me a kiss, and departed. I sat down to my Bible with my thoughts in a tumult. I should have been stupid indeed if I had not seen that Captain Gates liked to pay me little attentions, and his look as he handed me the honeysuckle that afternoon in the woods had made me shrink into myself, for I realized that he was not only interested in the subject of our conversation, but in me myself. I had honestly felt glad that he wished to talk on serious subjects, and I had been praying for him a great deal that day. Now Nelly's chaffing words had left their sting, and I felt humiliated by being discussed downstairs so freely before them all. My desires for Captain Gates' welfare were at an end. I felt I could never talk to him again.

But when I went down on my knees, and just spread the whole matter out in prayer, and then waited in silence till the quiet and peace came back into my heart, the case looked very different. And, turning over the leaves of my Bible, I

Amy Le Feuvre

was guided to this verse, 'As every man hath received the gift, even so minister the same one to another, as good stewards of the manifold grace of God.' Yes; I resolved that when opportunities were given to me of speaking a word for my Master, I would take them gladly, yet at the same time I would not seek to make them for myself, especially in connection with Captain Gates.

'Dwell deep!' I said to myself. 'I can let these little vexations and misunderstandings pass unnoticed; they are like the breezes on the surface of a lake. If I dwell below, I shall enjoy the calm.'

The next day was Sunday, and at three o'clock in the afternoon I found myself waiting in the vestry for my scholars. They were not long after me. First Roddy, with a shining face and a large bunch of asters from his mother's garden, which he presented to me with great pride; then two little girls in huge sun-bonnets, and very brown arms and legs, named Hetty and Polly Tyke; a very heavy, sleepy-looking boy about four years old, sucking a large piece of sugar-candy; and lastly Jim Carter and a big girl about his own age, whom he held by the hand.

'We thought you'd like if Kitty was to come; she's blind, you see, and has never been to no Sunday School, because no one will take charge of her; they runs off after a time, and then she comes to grief, she do!'

I was a little nonplussed, as I had only expected quite an infant class; but I made the best of it, and after singing a hymn that they all seemed to know I had a short prayer, and then settled down to a Bible story. I took Samuel's first call, made them each learn a little verse about it, and then began to talk to them. They were very quiet and listened almost breathlessly, but we had a few interruptions: Roddy suddenly nodded his head very violently towards me, and burst forth in the middle of my talk,—'I'll bring you a robin's egg to-morrer, a booful little egg for your breakfus! I'll go in at the big gates all by myself, and I'll knock at the big door with my stick, and then won't you be very 'stonished!'

I hushed him, and a few minutes after little Tommy Evans dropped his piece of sugar-candy, and in bending down to pick it up, overbalanced himself and fell with a crash to the ground; of course he howled, and I had to take him on my knee to pacify him. But these little incidents did not lessen their interest in the Bible story, and when I gave them each a little reward ticket at the close their delighted faces showed their appreciation of it all. The hour over, I dismissed them, and after promising to come again the next Sunday with several fresh scholars, the little ones scampered off. Jim politely offered to put the room tidy again, and whilst he was doing it I drew the blind girl out into the church porch and had a little talk with her. She told me her mother took in washing, and she helped her as much as she could. 'For father's been dead this five years, and grandfather's an old man, and has rheumatics so bad in his knee he can't do no work, so mother she keeps him; I wasn't always blind, I had scarlet fever when I was just on three years old, but oh, I does wish for my sight in the summer!'

'You poor child!' I said pityingly, 'you must long to see the flowers, I feel sure.'

'Teacher,' she said earnestly, 'I like that about Samuel; I shall try and say softly sometimes, "Speak, Lord, for Thy servant heareth." He will speak, won't He? I should like to hear His voice.'

'You will, Kitty, I know you will. God wants to have you for His servant. You give yourself to Him, and ask for His Holy

Amy Le Feuvre

Spirit to teach you day by day.'

This short conversation sent me home with a happy heart. I felt thankful that I had found some work, and I resolved to visit the parents of each child during the week.

It was a very different atmosphere I came into a short time later. Tea on Sunday afternoon was a time for visitors to drop in, and the conversation seemed to me always on the most frivolous subjects.

Constance and Mr. Stroud had escaped and gone away into the garden by themselves, and of course their engagement was being discussed as well as the gaieties of the coming week.

I got into a quiet corner and took my tea in silence, hoping I might be left unmolested, but this was not to be. A Miss Gordon, with a magnificent voice, was singing as I entered, and when she had finished Kenneth turned to me: 'Now, Goody Two-Shoes, give us something from your violin.'

He invariably addressed me by that name now, and I knew how vain it would be to protest against it.

'Oh yes, Miss Thorn,' said Miss Gordon, 'we have heard wonderful things of your playing; you are quite a genius, aren't you?'

'No,' I said, colouring a little, 'I am certainly not that, though I am very fond of it; I must ask you, I am afraid, to excuse my playing this afternoon.'

'Oh, please play; why won't you oblige us?'

'I never use my violin on Sunday.'

There was dead silence; then a Mrs. Parker, a young widow who had come with Miss Gordon, said, 'But, my dear Miss Thorn, play us something sacred, of course. I always consider the violin quite a Sunday instrument. In our village the chapel people have two going at every service they hold. You surely cannot think it wicked to play it on Sunday?'

No,' I said, 'I don't think it is *wicked*, but I would rather not do it. I am sure you will not press me.'

'She has just come back from Sunday School,' said Kenneth, looking across at me with a twinkle in his eye, 'and so she is doubly shocked with our levity. I assure you, Mrs. Parker, her religious scruples are such that I don't think she would pick a flower in the garden if you were to ask her to on the Sabbath!

I rose from my seat, for I had finished my tea, and pointing to a crimson rose in my waist-belt I said half laughing; 'I picked this as I came in this afternoon,' and then I left the room and went upstairs, where I had a nice quiet hour by myself. I felt quiet times alone were quite essential to me now, otherwise I seemed to almost lose touch with the unseen things that were so dear to me.

CHAPTER VI

ONLY A FRIEND

'Surely a woman's affection
Is not a thing to be asked for,
and had for only the asking?

—Longfellow

Wednesday evening came, and all went off to Lady Walker's except Hugh and myself. He seemed very rarely to go out with the others, and was generally up in London several nights a week. I had helped the girls to dress, and had done all I could for them before they went, but it had been a trying time. General Forsyth had hardly spoken to me since he knew my decision was final, and Mrs. Forsyth was continually referring to my foolishness. So I was relieved when they were out of the house, and quite enjoyed the quiet dinner with Hugh. He certainly exerted himself to be agreeable, and asked me if I would come upstairs and sit in his study after dinner.

'Bring your violin,' he said, 'and if you will play nicely to me I will treat you to a glimpse of the heavens through my telescope. It is a beautiful starry night.'

His study was a very comfortable-looking room, with a large bay window overlooking the open country, and I took up my position in front of it as I played to him. I did not know he was so fond of music; but as I laid my violin down I noticed how he was leaning back in his chair with a dreamy smile upon his face, and drawing in a long breath, he said,—

'Thank you. I think that's a better class of entertainment than what is going on at the Walkers' at present. A low-level life there, I consider, and one only marvels at men and women spending their whole existence in such trifles: time and talents utterly wasted, and powers of intellect used and abused in the foolish chit-chat of society!'

He spoke so contemptuously that I looked up in surprise.

'I think,' I said, 'every one must have something to fill their life. They are as much occupied in their gay sphere as you are in your literary one.'

'Or as you in your pious one! Quite true; and I suppose we each think our own sphere immeasurably superior to any other. I tell you honestly, I have a contempt for the frivolous one, and a pity for the religious. I look at both from a higher platform.'

'You place all your faith in man's intellect,' I said slowly; 'but "religious" people, as you call them, place their faith in the Creator of man's intellect. I don't think you are on a higher platform than they; you haven't got quite high enough.'

He made a movement of impatience in his chair, then relapsed into his natural supercilious manner.

'It is amusing to hear you air your views so dogmatically; if you were versed in some of the literature of the present day, and knew how many old-time notions and superstitions are disappearing under the full clear light of reason and science, you would not speak so positively. You must let me lend you a few books that may enlarge your thoughts and enlighten you on these subjects.'

'No, thank you,' I said quietly; 'you mustn't be vexed if I say again, you don't rise high enough; you read and study the works and production of men's brains, but I go by God's own Book, and that is beyond and above them all.'

Hugh laughed. 'I never argue with women, or I would show you how faulty your statements are. But never mind. I would rather see a girl take serious views of life than fritter it away as most do. You mean well, and live up to your light. Now would you like to have a look through my telescope?'

I assented; but I could not help wondering how much or how little Hugh really did believe. Nothing could be kinder than his explanations of the different planets and stars that we looked out upon, and for a full hour I was engrossed in gazing at various constellations above. I had always been interested in astronomy, and Hugh was very lucid as well as patient in giving me a great deal of fresh information. I listened and gazed breathlessly, and at last came away from the telescope with a deep-drawn breath of regret.

'It is so lovely; it seems to carry one quite away from earth altogether: the infinite space stretching away and away. Oh, Mr. Forsyth, you do not doubt the existence of God, do you?'

'No; I believe in a Supreme Being. I am not such an utter unbeliever as that.'

'I should hardly think any one who studied astronomy could believe that the universe was made by chance. Isn't there some spot in the Pleiades which is the centre of the whole solar system? I remember seeing some article about it once, and I like to think of heaven there.'

He smiled, but changed the conversation, and we did not touch on serious subjects again. When I prayed that night, I especially remembered Hugh; it seemed so sad to me that he was only using his intellect to try and discover flaws in the Bible, and prove to himself and others that some of the most important truths in Christianity were only popular superstitions.

Nelly had told me much about him; for though he kept himself aloof a great deal from the girls, every now and then he would unbend, and, as he had done this night, would take them into his study and interest them with his telescope and conversation.

But I resolved not to read any of his books. I felt I dared not wilfully go into such temptation; and when, as I was leaving him, he asked me if I would like the loan of a few, I answered, 'No, thank you, I would rather not. I am not a dissatisfied, restless soul that is seeking for the truth. I have found it, and am happy in it.'

'You are a very self-satisfied soul, at all events,' he said.

I coloured up, for I had been feeling a little self-righteous as I mentally condemned him for his free-thinking opinions.

'I ought not to be satisfied,' I said in a contrite voice, 'with self; but I am satisfied with Christ.'

And then I left him.

Nelly was very full of the delightful evening they had spent,

Amy Le Feuvre

when I saw her the next morning, and I listened and tried to take an interest in her account, for I knew how she loved to talk about such things; but I heard nothing to make me regret my choice.

'Captain Gates left us that afternoon. As he was wishing us all good-bye, he turned to me and said:

'You will see me over here in another three weeks, for I am coming to the dance here then, so this will not be a long good-bye.'

Then, as he shook hands with me, he lowered his voice, and said earnestly, 'I shall not forget our talks together, Miss Thorn. I have been most interested, and I honestly tell you, I should like to have the happiness and satisfaction that you get out of your religion. I don't know if I shall ever get it; but you will give me a thought sometimes, won't you?'

'If you read the Bible, I am sure you will find what you need there,' I said.

We were very quiet for the next week or two; I began visiting my Sunday scholars in their homes, and started reading-lessons with Jim. We went out into the fields, and under the shade of some old tree would spend many a quiet half-hour. He was so anxious and eager to learn that I did not find his dullness trying, and though progress seemed very slow, it was sure, for what he once learnt he did not easily forget. Jim's uncle, Roger Carter, was quite a character, and he dearly loved me to drop in and have a chat with him. He was a good old man, and generally asked me to have a bit of reading or a prayer with him before I left. And when he discovered that I played on the violin, nothing would pacify him until I had brought it down and given him a tune.

'Ah,' he said, drawing a long breath, 'that's something like moosic, that is. I know the right sort when I heers it. I've got a ear for it, though I've not the hands. I plays my toones on these 'ere boots and shoes.' And he laughed as he looked up at me through his shaggy eyebrows.

The day came for the Forsyths' dance. I had asked Mrs. Forsyth quietly if she would mind my keeping in my own room and not appearing at all; but this she would not hear of, and I felt myself that it would be a difficult thing to do. I longed to go away somewhere for a few days, and so miss it; but my old cousin in London had gone abroad, and I had very few old friends. So I determined to make no fuss about it, and trusted that I should be able to escape notice in the crowd, and slip away by myself when the dancing began. I told Nelly positively that if I was present I would not dance. She laughed at me, and assured me I would change my mind when the time came.

I did not realize what a large affair it would be, and I must honestly confess as the time drew near I felt a certain pleasurable excitement in all the preparations for it. A large marquee was put up on the lawn, and I with the others helped in decorating and draping it inside. A regimental band was coming, and Nelly assured me with pride,—

'Our autumn ball is the event of the year. You will see that everybody will be here.'

And so at last the evening arrived. Both Nelly and I were in soft white silk; and when Mrs. Forsyth came into my room to inspect my dress before going down, she said kindly,—

'You look very nice, child. Now I hope you are going to enjoy yourself like other girls, and not let silly scruples lead you into doing anything that will displease General Forsyth.'

Amy Le Feuvre

'I am not going to dance, Mrs. Forsyth,' I said, flushing as I spoke.

She left my room without replying, and then kneeling down, I asked to be kept and guided throughout the evening. I found great comfort in the verse, 'I pray not that Thou shouldest take them out of the world, but that Thou shouldest keep them from the evil.' And on my knees I asked that I might not only be kept from joining in the gaiety, but from wishing to join in it, for I felt how little I knew my own heart. All that day I had had longings to throw myself heart and soul into everything, as Nelly intended doing; and I found myself wondering if there would be very much harm in doing so.

An hour later and I was in the midst of it. The first one who made his way to me was Captain Gates.

'I want you to give me a waltz,' he said. 'We have danced together before, so don't say "No." I have been looking forward to it.'

I shook my head.

'I can see from your face, Captain Gates, that you know what my answer will be. I think you would be very surprised if I were to do it.'

'I assure you I shouldn't be,' he responded; 'there's no earthly difference in dancing now and dancing a week or two ago. It is the same partner and the same place. Come, don't make my evening an unpleasant one by refusing!'

'I should not do that in any case,' I answered; 'there are plenty of other partners in the room for you.'

'I will not dance with any of them if I cannot dance with you.'

I looked up in surprise; there was suppressed vehemence in his tone; he went on,—

'Will you come out upon the terrace with me? I—I want to speak to you.'

I hesitated, and wanted to refuse, but I had a longing to get out into the cool air, and I did not realize at the time what it might lead to.

So throwing a light shawl over my head I stepped out upon the terrace, and then suddenly he overwhelmed me with surprise and consternation by telling me that he cared for me, and asking if I could return his love.

'I am very, very sorry,' I faltered; 'but you have known me such a little while that I never dreamt of such a thing. I can hardly believe you are in earnest even now.'

'Do I look as if I were trifling?' he said earnestly. 'Miss Thorn, you have the making of me in your hands. I have led a useless kind of life up to the present, and I have for a long time been dissatisfied and restless about it. I see you have what I have not, and I want your help. I do want a good woman as my wife—I feel she could raise my life to a higher level, and you could do this for me.'

'I cannot,' I said gravely. 'No one can do that but God.'

He went on without heeding me,—

'Don't think I am asking you only to be my reformer—I would give you love in return. You don't know what you are

Amy Le Feuvre

to me! I cannot get your image out of my heart. Don't steel yourself against me, but try, do just try, to like me.'

'I like you as a friend very much,' I replied, trying to speak gently, for I could see he was very much moved. 'You have been most kind to me ever since I came; I am only so sorry that I cannot think of you in any other light.'

'A friend!' he exclaimed impetuously; 'I don't want that. Ah! Miss Thorn, you are so desirous of doing good and spending your life in ministering to others, and yet when an opportunity comes of really benefiting a human creature and of making him into a good man, you turn away in scorn. If you will have nothing to say to me, you will send me from bad to worse!'

'Oh, Captain Gates!' and tears that I could not keep back started to my eyes, 'you know it is not in scorn I am acting so. But it wouldn't be for our good if I were to say "Yes." I have not any love to give you, and I know myself better than you do. If I loved you, I would not dare to link my life with yours. Forgive me for saying it. I am not strong enough to lead you; I should be led by you. You do not know what a weak creature I am. As it is, I feel I am safe, for I put my trust in God, and He keeps me; but I would not dare to place myself in a position of temptation and then expect Him to keep me in it.'

'Really you must have a very low opinion of me. What kind of a life do you think I lead? I want to do better, I want to be an out-and-out Christian. And I want you to help me to become one.'

'Hilda! out here? I am so warm that I shall come and join you. How delicious the air is!'

It was Nelly who cut our conversation short, and I was very thankful to make my escape. I felt I must be alone, and hastened away to my own room.

CHAPTER VII

A FRESH ACQUAINTANCE

'I say
Just what I think, and
Nothing more or less.'

—Longfellow

I was not missed that night, and no one came near me. With my Bible on my knees, I felt quite convinced that I had acted rightly, and I was thankful that beyond a sincere liking for Captain Gates as a friend I had no other feeling to make my decision a hard matter. Inexperienced as I was, I knew no Christian ought to yoke themselves with another, with only the hope of helping them heavenwards in view. And I felt that if I were to love any one, it must be one who could help and lead me in the right way, and who was an older and a better Christian than I was myself. But I was sorry for Captain Gates, and wrote him a little note that same night, for I was afraid lest the interruption to our conversation should give him the excuse for continuing the subject when another opportunity offered itself, and that I wanted to avoid.

The next morning I went to Mrs. Forsyth's boudoir, and finding her alone told her of what had passed the night before. She was much surprised, and not altogether pleased.

'I ought to have looked after you better,' she said, 'but Captain Gates has seemed more like a brother to my girls. He was brought up with the boys, and has looked upon this as his second home. I noticed, of course, how attentive he was to you; but it is his way with most fresh acquaintances, and I never dreamed of it leading to anything serious. Why, he has no prospects beyond his pay and a trifling allowance from his father! What could he be dreaming of?'

I listened, but said nothing, only wondered at the different views people took of things. Mrs. Forsyth's reason for my refusal of him was so very far apart from mine.

The ball was a theme of conversation for many days after, and I was thankful that my absence from it had been so little noticed. But, as time went on, my life seemed to get very difficult. I think I had naturally a bright disposition, and so in the first freshness of my surroundings did not mind the little disagreeables attending my 'strait-laced views,' as Nelly called them. When Captain Gates had left us, our gaiety did not cease; I seemed to be continually in opposition to my guardian, and after bearing a good deal of grave displeasure from him, and light scorn from the rest, I was finally left in peace to go my way alone, with the sense of being in perpetual disgrace, and being shunned and avoided by most of the girls' friends. This I could not help feeling acutely—I longed to be friends with every one; and many a tear was shed in the privacy of my own room, as I would see a merry party leave the house bound on some excursion—perhaps a simple water picnic—to which I had not been asked, on account of my 'peculiar ideas.' Then it was I sought to 'dwell deep,' and found increasing comfort in studying my little Bible. I was not dull, for I visited much in the village. My Sunday class increased, and my little scholars were a perpetual source of enjoyment to me. I went for walks with Violet and her governess, and when feeling lonely would often take my violin up to my room and enjoy an hour or two there in quiet. Sometimes Hugh would ask me to come in and play to him, and as the evenings drew in I often went to him for an hour before dinner. He really was fond of music, and would lean back in his chair and thoroughly enjoy it. I tried to make myself as pleasant to every one as I could: I helped Mrs. Forsyth in her gardening, which was her particular hobby; I ran errands for the girls, and made a point of obliging them in every way possible; I practised my violin with Violet, and was always ready for an outdoor scramble with her when Miss Graham was not able to accompany us; and in filling up my days with these occupations I learnt to be content and happy.

'You are a good little thing, Hilda,' Nelly said one day to me, as I was handing her back a pair of gloves I had been mending for her. 'I sometimes think we are very horrid to you. I wish you weren't so awfully religious; but I will say this for you, that you practise what you preach, and your religion seems to suit you. I am sure, though you haven't half the fun that I have, you always look as bright and jolly as you can be. How do you manage it?'

'I try to "dwell deep,"' I said; and Nelly laughingly rejoined as she left me,—

'I am sure you are deeper than I am. I like to skim the surface as I go through life; one gets the cream that way.'

It was a bright October morning. I had been picking some late roses on the lawn close to the house, and with my hands full of those and some lovely sprays of red and gold-coloured leaves was just entering the hall door, when a strange voice made me turn round.

'Is Mrs. Forsyth at home?'

It was a lady who spoke, in clear, brisk tones; she was not very young, and wore a severely plain dress: a round felt hat like a man's, with two or three crow's feathers stuck in carelessly at the side, a thick pair of leather gauntlets, and carried a walking stick in her hand.

I was answering in the affirmative, when suddenly down came her hand on my shoulder.

'Are you Hilda Thorn?'

'Yes,' I said, quietly meeting a searching look from two keen dark eyes under very thick eyebrows.

'And you are indeed, I hear, a veritable thorn in the side of my poor sister. I am glad to have met you. Now take me to her.'

Her quick, imperative tones awed me. I had heard Nelly talk about an aunt of theirs, a Miss Rayner, who was a strong-minded and peculiar woman, and I rightly conjectured that this must be she.

We found Mrs. Forsyth in her own sitting-room, busy with accounts, and I fancied she did not look well pleased at the advent of the visitor.

'Well, Helen,' she said, rising from her seat, 'you are home again, then. I thought you were still in America. This is quite a surprise.'

'I don't take long over business, and I am not one to let the grass grow under my feet. I have been making acquaintance with this young person. Why, Maria, she is a mere baby!'

Amy Le Feuvre

I beat a retreat hastily, and finding Nelly practising a song in the drawing-room, told her of the arrival.

'Aunt Helen! my goodness! won't mother be in a fuss! She pays us periodical visits to set us all straight. Isn't she a cure, Hilda? I'm always expecting to see her walk in rigged out in a sporting costume—knickerbockers and all. She wears a greatcoat in winter exactly like a man's.'

'She has a handsome face,' I said, 'and I like her short grey hair; it seems to suit her. She must be quite six foot, Nelly, isn't she?'

'Yes, half an inch over, I think. What did she say to you?'

'She told your mother I was a mere baby.'

Nelly burst out laughing. 'That's better than being called an empty-pated noodle, as I was, the last time I was addressed by her. Now I wonder if she is going to stay to lunch; did she say?'

'I did not hear her. Where does she live?'

'Only about fifteen miles from here, but we do not often meet. She is quite a character. Do you know what her hobby is? Rearing poultry. She keeps what she calls a "chicken farm," and sends her eggs and fowls up to London. In the winter she uses incubators, and has broods of chickens all the year round. Her farm is quite a sight worth seeing. I believe she has lots of visitors from all parts, and she prides herself upon having all the latest improvements. She has just been over to Chicago about an incubator; they are always adding improvements, she says, and she went over to see it properly worked.'

'But does she do this from mercenary motives?' I asked.

'Oh no. She is very comfortably off; it is just her hobby, but I believe she makes money over it. She is a clever woman, and hates society. She must do something with her life, I suppose. I believe she has a love story, but mother will never tell; she always says, "It was not for the lack of suitors that your aunt has remained single."'

I was interested in this account of Miss Rayner, and when we met at luncheon I found my eyes continually wandering in her direction. She talked well, and was most amusing, though her sarcastic speeches and scornful curl of the lip rather spoilt the conversation, I thought.

She took no notice of me, and so I was greatly astonished, when she was bidding us all good-bye shortly after lunch, to see her give a quick nod at me and say,

'I shall see you shortly. You are coming over to stay with me the end of next week. Don't bring a lot of evening toggery, for you will not see a soul except myself.'

Seeing my surprised looks, Mrs. Forsyth said,—

'I have not asked her if she would like to go yet.'

'Oh, she will come fast enough,' responded Miss Rayner sharply. 'She has been listening quietly and drawing her own conclusions about me during luncheon, and she thinks I am queer, but that I am different to most folks. Novelty has a charm for the young. *Au revoir*, Miss Thorn.'

She gave me a little mocking bow, kissed Mrs. Forsyth, waved her hand to the others, and was gone before I could recover from my surprise at this sudden announcement.

Amy Le Feuvre

I turned to Mrs. Forsyth for an explanation, but she merely said,

'Miss Rayner has invited you over to her place for a week or two. Of course it remains with you whether you would like to go or not. Nelly has stayed with her once or twice; so she can tell you whether you will be likely to enjoy yourself there.'

'But she never asked me, mother,' said Nelly. 'I only went there in a convalescent state after an attack of measles. She must have taken a wonderful fancy to Hilda to ask her.'

Visions of my Sunday scholars floated before me, and I said hesitatingly,—

'I don't know that I care about going, Mrs. Forsyth. She is a perfect stranger to me, and I am quite happy here.'

'I think the change will be good for you,' said Mrs. Forsyth, 'and it has come at the right time, for I think of taking the two girls up to London for three weeks. Miss Forsyth, their aunt, has asked us. She extended the invitation to you; but unless you behave differently there to what you do with us, I really could not undertake to have the charge of you. She lays herself out for the pleasure of young people in her house, and you could hardly accept her hospitality if you refused to take part in every entertainment that was provided for you.'

'No,' I said quietly, 'I am afraid I should only be a wet blanket if I went. I will go to Miss Rayner's if you wish, Mrs. Forsyth. Perhaps you would rather I went to her than stay quietly at home?'

'I certainly should!'

And so the matter was settled. Mrs. Forsyth and the girls left the room, but I stood for a moment at the window looking out into the garden. I felt the sting of Mrs. Forsyth's words; she did not often hint so plainly what a trouble I was to her, and though I knew it was true, it gave me a lonely, desolate feeling, and I wondered how I could always bear it. Tears came to my eyes, and then suddenly Kenneth's voice broke in,

'Crying, Goody? What's the matter?'

I had not noticed he was in the room, and hastily controlled myself. His light, bantering tone jarred upon me, but I answered, trying to laugh, 'Nothing; I am silly, that is all.'

'I don't think you can want to go to wicked London, do you?' he pursued, as he threw himself back into an easy chair and surveyed me meditatively. 'Do you think you are being banished to Miss Rayner's as a punishment?'

'Of course not. I—I am only sorry that I vex your mother so.'

'You have the remedy in your own hands. But I suppose you get a good deal of pleasure out of the consciousness of your own superiority to us all, and that solaces and supports you through everything.'

'You know that is not so!' I said, and my tone was indignant.

He laughed. 'You mustn't get angry, you know; that is not saintly. Are you frightened of our respected aunt?'

'No, not frightened, but I am not fond of making fresh acquaintances, and sometimes I feel that there is no place for me here; if only I had a home of my own!'

Amy Le Feuvre

'I think I can manage that for you,' was Kenneth's reply. 'Let me send a line to Gates; I will tell him you are relenting.'

I ignored this speech, and continued: 'You know what I mean. If my parents had lived, it would have been so different. Not that I have anything to complain of. No one could be kinder than General and Mrs. Forsyth. I am only sorry that I have disappointed them so!'

Kenneth was silent for a moment, then he said cheerfully, 'Look here! I am not going up to town, so I promise to ride over and see you while you are with my aunt. Then you can tell me if she is bullying you. You need not stay there if you do not like it.'

I laughed.

'Perhaps I shall like her so much that I shall not want to come back here. But I shall be very glad to see you if you come.'

CHAPTER VIII

DRAWN TOGETHER

'As we meet and touch each day
The many travellers on our way,
Let every such brief contact be
A glorious helpful ministry.'

I have a very pleasant recollection of my arrival at Miss Rayner's home. It was a lovely afternoon, bright and sunny, with a touch of frost in the air, when I reached the little country station. There was a trap waiting for me outside, in charge of a garrulous old coachman who was quite a character. When he had seen to my luggage and wrapped a fur rug round me, I noticed him taking a sidelong glance at me, and then he commenced, 'You're a fresh h'arrival here, I reckon, miss. We don't so h'often have young lady visitors.'

'You have had one of the Miss Forsyths,' I said.

'Well—yes, we have, h'and I don't see much harm in her. She's flighty, but she's young, h'and time will mend that. H'are you closely h'intimated with the mistress?'

I smiled. 'No, I cannot say that,' I answered, 'but I hope to be soon.'

Amy Le Feuvre

He shook his head doubtfully. 'She's no h'ordinary female. Hi'm no great lover of the weaker sex, but hi'll say this for Miss Helen, h'and I've known her from the time I took her h'out h'on her first pony, she's a deal more sensibility than many h'of h'us men! I h'often says to Susan, who h'is a poor h'useless body with a very long tongue, h'and it's h'only the mistress's kindness to keep such h'an h'old pottering body h'on, for she's h'always making an h'ado about nothing. I says, "Susan, the mistress h'is h'almost h'equal to a master," and that's saying a good deal. She holds herself high, and she's h'impatient like of women folks; but she has a proper respect for me that has been in the family so long, and though it is laughable how she thinks she has me in leading-strings and manages me h'entirely, I h'affords her that pleasure, h'and goes my h'own way. Ah! She's a fine woman, Miss Helen is!'

With these and similar remarks he beguiled my drive, and though I smiled at the self-importance of his tone, I could tell that he was an attached and faithful servant. We stopped at length at a gate, drove through it up a short avenue of limes, and then came to one of the prettiest old-fashioned farmhouses that I have ever been in. It was a long, low gable-roofed house, with latticed casements, and autumn-tinted creepers covering the old grey stone and porch. The door was open, and two large dogs darted out to welcome us. When I stepped inside a cheery-looking old woman appeared in a very large cap and apron.

'Miss Thorn, isn't it, my dear? The mistress was called out on a matter of business, and she asked me to make you comfortable. Come this way, miss; you'll be glad of a bit of a fire after your cold drive?'

She led me through the square hall, wainscoted up to the ceiling with old oak, and having an oaken staircase with very thick balustrades on either side going up from the middle of it, into a long, low room which, with crimson druggeting on the floor, and the same coloured curtains to the windows, looked very cosy and bright in the firelight.

She left me saying she would bring in tea, and I, seating myself in an easy chair by the fire, spread out my feet in front of the blaze, and looked about me curiously. Comfort certainly was more studied than elegance in this room. No flimsy draperies or works of art adorned the chairs and couches. A small square oak table stood in the centre of the room. On it was a beautiful chrysanthemum, some magazines and papers, and a pair of riding gloves thrown carelessly down. Two large crimson-covered couches occupied the deep recesses on either side of the fire place. A well-filled bookcase stood opposite between the pretty casement windows, and a stand of ferns at the end of the room was in front of another window, through which I could catch a glimpse of some distant hills and the setting sun disappearing behind them. The walls, like the hall, were wainscoted with old oak, but some beautiful water-colours and old china relieved their somewhat sombre hue.

The old servant soon returned, wheeling in a round table up to the fire, and bringing in a tempting-looking tea with plenty of hot cakes and scones.

'Help yourself, miss,' she said, in a motherly sort of tone; 'the mistress may be out some time yet. I hope you didn't find the open trap cold. John, he will have his way sometimes, but I said to him you would have been better with the closed wagonette. I hope John didn't make too free, miss? He has a longer tongue, I tell him, than any woman's; but he has seen a deal of life! He was London born and bred, and goes up every year to visit his friends there. He's getting old now, as I am myself; but though he speaks sharp, he's as easy to be

Amy Le Feuvre

managed as a baby. Any one can twist him round with their little finger, so long as they just flatter him a bit.'

How I laughed to myself when she left me, and wondered when they both got together whose tongue was the longest!

I enjoyed the tea provided for me, and liked the quiet and solitude—such a contrast to the Forsyths' afternoon meal. Then, as no one came, a sudden longing took possession of me to try my violin. The dusky twilight, and the fire flickering over the quaint, old-fashioned room, seemed to bring me into a world of fancy.

I had my violin with me, as I would never trust my case in any other hand but mine, and so, slipping off my jacket, I was soon in a dream, playing on and on without a thought of my present surroundings.

I don't know how long I played, but as the last note died away a brisk voice said from the further side of the room,—

'Bravo! I like to hear any one play without being conscious of listeners.'

I started. It was Miss Rayner, leaning back in an easy chair, who spoke; but when I apologised for making myself so at home, she said sharply, 'Tut, child! No company manners here, or I shall wish you away. Now I want some tea. How long have you been here?'

I told her, and then she said,

'And what do you think of my invitation? Are you pleased to be here?'

'Yes, I think I am,' I said honestly. 'I was a little shy about it at first; but now I have come, it seems so restful and quiet.'

'That's because I was out,' she said, with a short laugh; 'but I will allow it is a quieter house than the one you have left. When do they leave for town?'

'To-morrow.'

'And are you longing to be with them?'

There was a quizzical gleam in her eye, as my gaze met hers.

'No,' I said a little gravely; 'they would rather be without me, and I should not be happy with them.'

'You evidently do not shake in well with them. Ah, well! I will not catechise you too closely the first evening. I shall soon find out what your special fads and crotchets are. Now, would you like to come upstairs to your room? I dine at half-past seven, and it is nearly seven now. Have you made friends with Susan? I call her my maid-of-all-work—she was my mother's maid years ago, and has stuck to me ever since. I have a very small establishment, as you perceive. Susan is house, parlour, and lady's-maid all in one, with only a young girl to help her. John is coachman, groom, and gardener combined, and an old cook completes our household.'

'But who helps in the—the poultry farm?' I asked, as I followed her up the old-fashioned staircase.

'I keep a man and a boy for that part of the business; they sleep out of the house.'

She led me into a pretty little room with a very deep window seat. It was furnished simply, but comfortably, though quite devoid of all knick-knacks.

Amy Le Feuvre

When I was alone, I just knelt down and asked that even here I might be given some work to do, and, above all, that I might not be ashamed to own my Master.

Miss Rayner appeared at dinner in a severe black silk made perfectly plain; she glanced at my lighter costume as we took our seats at the table, and said,—

'How many of those flimsy gowns have you brought with you? I told you I should have no company.'

'I have only one other with me,' I replied meekly.

'I think girls spend more money on evening dresses than any other object, and generally look the worse for them,' she continued. 'Why on earth women shouldn't have a universal dress suit, like the men, I can't imagine.'

'You do not mean the same as the men's?' I said, laughing.

'The same in colour, if not in cut,' she said briskly. 'Black and white would be suitable for young and old, and the variety of face would be more noticeable, instead of as now, the variety of dress.'

And then she turned to other subjects, giving me an amusing account of her last visit to Chicago, and the people she had been introduced to there.

When dinner was over we went back to the drawing-room, and without further preface she said,—

'And now just tell me why you are giving my poor dear sister such trouble? It's enough to turn her hair grey, from her own account!'

Her tone was mocking, and I hesitated in complying with her request.

'Are you afraid of me?' she said, with a little laugh, after a minute's silence.

I looked her full in the face. 'No, I don't think I am; but I am afraid you will not understand.'

'My intellect may not be quite so keen and bright as yours, but if you try to use very simple language, perhaps I may be able to grasp your meaning.'

I coloured, and said confusedly, 'I am very sorry I am vexing Mrs. Forsyth so. I did not know when I came to live with General Forsyth that it would be so difficult. I don't care for gaiety, and don't wish to be drawn into it; and they want me to be the same as their daughters. It is their kindness that makes it so hard to hold out against their wishes.'

'And are you living only to please yourself?'

'I hope not,' I said slowly, as I took in the drift of her question; 'it is because I don't want to live for self that I feel it right to act so.'

Miss Rayner smiled a little contemptuously, I fancied.

'Oh, you young girls!' was all she said; but her tone silenced me.

After a few minutes, she said: 'And when did you come to the conclusion that you had a soul above the frivolities of this world?'

'Does that conclusion seem very absurd to you,

Amy Le Feuvre

Miss Rayner?'

She looked at me with an odd kind of smile. 'I believe you could be a little spitfire if you liked,' she said. 'You must remember I have lived a little longer in the world than you have. And I have met with young girls of something the same stamp as yourself, who ran away from home duties to visit in the slums, and because they despise men of the world, lavish all their love and adoration on a wishy-washy curate, who very often encourages them, and then gives them the slip in the end, sending them back to their homes sadder and wiser women. My sister has cause for thankfulness that there is no curate in her parish.'

'Miss Rayner, I don't think I quite deserve that,' I said.

She laughed. 'I am very rude and plain-spoken. You must put up with that if you come to stay with me. I did promise not to catechise you the first evening, didn't I? But the temptation proves too strong. I have had a lot of disagreeable business to-day, and now I feel I want relaxation and amusement.'

'Why have *you* given up going out into society?' I asked.

'Ah! Now you are turning the tables on me. But I have lived my life—you have yours yet to come. Can you give me any clear reason why you should be different to the Forsyths? Is it a matter of principle? If so, what is the principle?'

'"Be not conformed to this world,"' I said, in a low voice, but a steady one; '"Come out from among them, and be ye separate." Those are two commands I am trying to obey, Miss Rayner.'

'Why?' was the curt inquiry.

'Because I belong to Christ, and I want to carry out His wishes.'

'I don't think Christ shunned society. If I remember my Bible rightly, He did quite the reverse.'

'He would not have been found in the fashionable Roman Court society,' I said. 'I don't know much of the world, Miss Rayner; perhaps that is why I feel, if I went right into every sort of gaiety I should not be able to stop myself. I know I should become so fascinated and engrossed that I should think of nothing else. Don't you think it very engrossing? When you went out yourself, didn't you find it so?'

'I don't believe I have been put through my catechism so for years,' was Miss Rayner's reply. 'I reserve to myself the right of asking questions. And so you try to make your life one of rigid self-denial? It won't last long, child. You are only human like the rest of us, and the reaction will come, as I have seen it in scores of cases before.'

I said nothing.

She continued, after a pause:—

'You can't be happy leading such a life. It is not natural; and it must be a constant source of fret to yourself and those with whom you live.'

'But I am very happy, Miss Rayner—I really am. I have what satisfies my heart, and any amount of worldly pleasure never does that, does it? It is a difficult life to lead with the Forsyths, but I am helped to "dwell deep," and I am quite content.'

'And what friends have you?' Miss Rayner asked, her dark,

Amy Le Feuvre

piercing eyes fixed intently on my face.

'Well,' I said slowly, 'I have no special friends. I like Nelly and Violet very much, but Nelly has her own friends, and Violet is busy with her lessons. Most of the girls who come to the house of course find me rather slow, and leave me alone, but I am getting accustomed to that.'

'It won't last,' Miss Rayner said again; and then she asked me to play to her on my violin.

I did so, and she lay back in her chair, listening with half-closed eyes; but when I put my instrument down I again encountered her earnest gaze.

'You are a pretty little thing,' she said abruptly; 'I suppose that is no news to you?'

'I have not often been told so,' I said, flushing, and half laughing at her bluntness.

'It is no thanks to you that you are made so,' she said. 'I have no patience with people who are possessed with good looks; they invariably take the credit of their beauty to themselves, and are quite insufferable with all their airs and graces. I don't say this is the case with you, for I have not seen enough of you to tell yet. Now I am going to read, so you will be left in peace for a little. Would you like a magazine?'

There was no more talk between us that night. At half-past ten Miss Rayner rose and wished me good-night.

'I breakfast at half-past eight punctually,' she said; 'so you will like to retire now, I expect.'

And this I did, wondering, when I reached my room, what it

was that so attracted me towards Miss Rayner; for, in spite of her blunt manner and tone, I really had taken a liking to her, and was glad that I was going to see more of her.

CHAPTER IX

QUIET DAYS

'The slow, sweet hours that bring us all things good.'

—Tennyson

The next morning, after breakfast, Miss Rayner took me all over her chicken farm. It was most interesting to me, as I had never seen anything of the sort before. All the houses and contrivances for the chickens, from the time they left their egg-shells, were so perfect in every little detail, and the incubators I thought charming. A brood of little chicks were just hatched, but I could not help expressing my regret to Miss Rayner that they had no proper mother.

'They must miss such a lot,' I said; 'it seems such a desolate state to be in.'

'We never miss what we have not been accustomed to,' Miss Rayner said briskly. 'Much better have no mother than a bad one, and hens are not better than most folks—they very often ill-treat their young.'

I saw, from the way she went about and superintended everything, that her whole heart was with her poultry, and she was one to do all that came to her hand both thoroughly and well. Her servants seemed devoted to her, though I heard her scolding her outdoor man so severely that I wondered he stood it as meekly as he did.

I soon became quite at home, and enjoyed my new life immensely. I was left pretty much to myself in the morning, but in the afternoon Miss Rayner would often invite me out for a long walk or drive. She rode a great deal, and persuaded me to accompany her on a very quiet chestnut mare.

I had taken riding lessons at school, but had not had much opportunity of riding since, and the Forsyths never seemed to have a horse to spare. It was a great pleasure to me now, and I could not but enjoy Miss Rayner's society. She was a cultivated, well-read woman, and her conversation was very different to that to which I had been accustomed. She made me feel my own ignorance on many subjects, and I was glad to read the books and reviews she placed in my hands.

One evening she had given me a fresh book, dealing with some of the questions of the present day, and had said that she would like me to study it, for the writer was a clever and rising author.

I read on for some time in silence, and then I put it down.

'Is it too deep for you?' she asked.

'No,' I replied; 'but I don't like it.'

'I am surprised. There is such a decided religious tone in it that I thought it would just suit you.'

'It is just that tone I don't like. It represents some of the Bible truths so unfairly.'

'In what way?'

'In speaking of God's justice—'

'Please explain,' she said, as I faltered.

'Justice is not cruelty, Miss Rayner. I suppose he holds the same views that so many seem to hold. And even in novels now that you get at a circulating library you constantly come across the same thing—a kind of contempt for the "old, narrow doctrines," as they call them, bringing down God's standard to theirs, and condemning what they cannot understand.'

Miss Rayner laughed.

'You are getting hot over their iniquities. I did not know you were such a critical young person.'

'I can't bear the Bible being made light of,' I said. 'They cut away and put their own interpretation on the most solemn truths. Do you agree with this man, Miss Rayner?'

'In the face of such severe criticism, I should be bold to say I did,' was the laughing reply; then she added, more seriously, 'I don't really know what I do believe. Perhaps you would be shocked at some of my theories. I never trouble my head about doctrines; a man's life is more important than his creed.'

'And what kind of a life do you believe in?' I asked.

'An upright, honourable life, in which all lying and humbug would not find a place. A life spent for the good of one's fellow-creatures is the noblest one, but few attain to that. I think we ought to leave some the better for our influence when we depart this life.'

'And then?' I asked.

She shrugged her shoulders. '"Sufficient unto the day is the evil thereof." The present is what we have to deal with, not the future. Don't look so shocked, child. If you question me so closely, what am I to do? I am not an unbeliever. I go to church every Sunday morning, and, as you see, I keep up the old custom of family prayers once a day. Don't judge other people as heathen because they may not think exactly the same as yourself.'

I said no more. I felt too young and inexperienced to argue with a woman of such a stamp as Miss Rayner. She would lean back in her chair, and look and listen to me with an amused twinkle in her eyes; but as for being convinced of the truth by anything that I said, that, I knew, was a moral impossibility. Yet, when I went to my room that night, I prayed earnestly for her, and felt more than ever the comfort that what was impossible to man was easy and possible to God, and the Holy Spirit Himself could convince her of her need of a Saviour.

I was a little troubled lest, through cowardice, I had not made as good a use of the opportunity as I might have done; so the next morning, at breakfast, I said to her,—

'Miss Rayner, I have been thinking over our conversation last night. Do you think doing good to our fellow-creatures is all that God requires of us? Is He Himself not to have a place in our life? What do you think of words like these, "Thou hast created all things, and for Thy pleasure they are and were created"?'

'Now, look here,' she said good-naturedly, 'I am not going to be preached to. The chief thing that made me take to you was, that you were not a prig, with all your extreme devotedness. And I will not enter into religious discussions. I might disturb your faith, and I don't want to do that. Keep your religion to yourself, and live it out, child, if you want to impress others. I am sick of cant and humbug—be real and true, and you are sure to commend your views to others, but you will never do it by preaching at them.'

I coloured up. 'I didn't mean to preach,' I began.

'You felt it was on your conscience to say more to me. Oh, I know all about it! I can read your face like a book, and you took about ten minutes to make up your mind to do it.'

I could not help laughing at her tone, but said no more, as I saw how useless it would be.

It was a few days after this that Kenneth made his appearance. He rode up to the door just as we were sitting down to luncheon.

'What do you want?' asked Miss Rayner sharply, as she made him welcome at the table. 'I am not accustomed to visits from you.'

'No,' Kenneth said, laughing; 'I only came to see how Goody Two-Shoes was getting on, and whether she wants to come home again.'

'I am very happy here, thank you,' I said.

'I was not aware that the arrangement of her affairs was in your hands,' Miss Rayner remarked drily.

Kenneth laughed again good-humouredly. 'Well, you see, my

father is away, and I am acting as his representative. What do you think of her, aunt? Has she been trying to convert you yet?'

Miss Rayner's eyes sparkled a little as she looked across at me. 'I am not going to tell tales,' she said. 'We understand each other, I think—at any rate, we are trying to.'

'I am afraid she has not had sufficient scope at our house, for we are too many for her,' Kenneth pursued; 'the only one who was amenable to her influence was Captain Gates. I really believe he was quite willing, only she wouldn't do it for him, when it came to the point.'

'Oh, hush, Kenneth!' I exclaimed. 'Please don't talk so; you know how I dislike it.'

'I am afraid Gates has lost his chance,' Kenneth continued, with one of his provoking smiles. 'I met him last week, Goody, and what do you think he was doing? Now don't look so indifferent, for, remember, if he goes to the dogs, it will be you who has driven him there. He was packing his things up for Monte Carlo. And he is going to propose to the first heiress that he comes across, for he is desperately hard up just now.'

I felt my cheeks get hot, and I knew that Miss Rayner's eyes were scanning me closely.

'How is Violet?' I asked. 'Isn't she feeling rather lonely?'

'I never set eyes on her,' was the brotherly reply, 'except that before I got off this morning she came rushing out with all sorts of messages to you. I told her I shouldn't remember half. One was that she wanted you back, I think; the other, that Miss Graham had taken your precious Sunday class, and had found it so entertaining that she was going to try it again.'

'Oh, I am so glad!' I exclaimed. 'I was hoping she would; and is she going to give Jim a reading-lesson in the week, do you know?'

'That I can't tell you.'

After luncheon, Miss Rayner went down to the village on some errand, and then Kenneth inquired, 'Is she treating you well?'

'Of course,' I replied; 'she is most kind, and I am enjoying myself very much.'

'What on earth do you do with yourself all day in this out-of-the-way hole? Have you seen a single visitor since you have been here?'

'Not one,' I said, laughing; 'and for myself, I would just as soon be without them.'

'We are awfully slow at home just now,' Kenneth said; 'Hugh is as grumpy and cross as two sticks. I dine out whenever I can, and shoot everything I come across in the day-time. I even condescend to rabbits, if there's nothing better on hand. I think we shall have the house pretty full when the girls come back. Amongst other people, Hugh is asking a new crony of his, some scientific fellow whom he raves about.'

'I never heard him rave about anybody or anything!' I remarked.

'It is raving for him, when he tells you that his chum is thought no end of by different celebrities, and that he considers it an honour to have him under our unworthy roof —or words to that effect. Mother will be delighted to have him, as he is unmarried, and has a big estate somewhere.'

'Have you heard from Nelly?' I asked, changing the subject, as I did not like his sneering tone.

'Had a letter from her yesterday; she and Constance are going at it night and day. I say, Goody, how much longer are you going to stay here? Couldn't you tell the aunt you have had enough of it, and come back? It is too slow for anything just now. I promise you some nice little treats if you come. We will go up the river—you and I—and we shall have it all our own way, for there will be nobody to interfere with us.'

'I have promised to stay here till Mrs. Forsyth comes back,' I said.

'Oh, bother your promise! Say you found it too slow, and couldn't stand it any longer.'

'But I don't find it slow,' I said, looking at him full in the face. 'I think I like Miss Rayner's society better than yours.'

Kenneth looked quite taken aback at first, and then we both laughed together.

'It's true,' I persisted.

'I don't believe it; I shall give you a dose of my society to-day, for I shall stay on to dinner here. What shall we do this afternoon?'

'Miss Rayner does not expect you to stay on,' I said, 'for she wished you good-bye before she went out just now.'

Amy Le Feuvre

'I know she did, but I intend to stay, all the same.'

And this he did, telling Miss Rayner when she came in that there was no dinner at home, Hugh was in town, and he was sure she would offer him further hospitality.

Kenneth could be very amusing when he liked, and he certainly brought a fresh element into our quiet life. He asked me to play on my violin after dinner, and when I had finished he turned to Miss Rayner and said, 'That is Goody's strong forte—that instrument of hers. She could charm a man's soul away by some of her strains!' And then he took his leave.

There was silence between us for some time after his departure. I thought Miss Rayner was reading, and though I was professedly doing the same, my thoughts kept wandering off to Captain Gates. I wondered if I was responsible for his going back to his old reckless life. He had told me once what a snare gambling had been to him, and how much he wanted to give it up. This visit to Monte Carlo would plunge him into the midst of it again.

I was startled out of my reverie by Miss Rayner's voice saying, 'What pictures are you seeing in the fire, child?'

I looked up. 'I was only thinking,' I said.

'So I suppose. Who is this Captain Gates that Kenneth mentioned?'

I coloured. How often she seemed to read my thoughts! 'A friend of Kenneth who often comes to stay with the Forsyths.'

'And what has he to do with you, or you with him?'

I hesitated, then said in a low voice, 'He wanted me to marry him, and I couldn't!'

'Why not?'

'I—I didn't care enough for him, and we should not have suited each other. He leads a very gay life.'

'But I suppose he vowed he would give all that up?'

'Yes, he did; but I don't think he would have done so.'

And then, encouraged by a softening in her tone and manner, I told Miss Rayner all, asking her at the end if she did not think I had acted rightly.

'Quite right,' she said emphatically; 'but be thankful you were not head over ears in love with him, for your decision would have cost you something then.'

She spoke with such intense feeling that I could not help thinking there must be something behind her words, especially when she continued in low, earnest tones: 'Better go through life lonely and single, than tie yourself to a man whose aim and object in life is directly contrary to yours. There can be only misery for both if you act otherwise. And cut the connection at once for his sake, more than for your own. It is only prolonging the agony.'

I did not speak, and then, with a short laugh, Miss Rayner seemed to recover herself. 'What am I saying? Perhaps some day I may tell you a chapter in my life, child—but not now. You have not had to go through such a sharp ordeal as I have. I am afraid there is nothing for it but a curate for you. Holding your present views, you would find no pleasure in a man of the world.'

'Surely every one is not bound to have a husband?' I said, half laughing, half vexed with her light, mocking tone.

'I should say you were sure to have one,' she retorted; 'perhaps your views will melt away when you come across some one that you really fancy.'

I shook my head, but dropped the subject, wondering, with a girlish curiosity, what Miss Rayner's life story was.

CHAPTER X

LONG AGO

'Ah! changeless through the changing vein
The ghostly whisper rings between
The dark refrain of "might have been."'

Circumstances helped to bring about the recital of that story sooner than I had expected. About ten days later, I started out one afternoon with Miss Rayner for a ride. I was not on the chestnut mare this time, but on Rawdon, Miss Rayner's special favourite, and the one she always rode herself. It was a mark of great favour her allowing me to try him.

It was a pleasant day for a ride, and when we got up on a bit of the moor it delighted me. Suddenly, without any warning, a pack of hounds dashed by, followed closely by the huntsmen. 'Pull your horse in, child!' Miss Rayner exclaimed excitedly; 'he is an old hunter.'

It was easy to say, but quite impossible, I found, to act upon. Rawdon threw up his head, his nostrils quivering with excitement, and then bolted, and I found myself utterly powerless to check his course.

'Keep your seat, and give him his head,' were the words I

heard from Miss Rayner as I rapidly left her in the distance.

'And keep cool,' I said to myself, knowing I should require all my nerve. In a few minutes I was in the midst of the hunt, to my great perplexity, and, passing most of the riders, Rawdon galloped on to the front. It had been a fortunate thing for me that the bit of moor we were on was on the level; but now I saw, to my consternation, the hounds were making for some fields adjoining, and Rawdon was carrying me straight towards a five-barred gate. I had practised leaps in a riding-school, but never since, and my heart sank within me. I put up a quick prayer as we reached it; Rawdon took it without the slightest difficulty, and to my surprise I found myself still on his back.

'It will be the finish at that next copse, I expect,' a gentleman called out excitedly, as his horse vainly tried to keep up with mine. 'Look out for that hedge in front,' he added; 'it's a nasty leap—there is a wide ditch the other side.'

What could I say or do? He evidently did not see that my horse had obtained complete mastery of me. I set my teeth, and drew my breath as we approached it. Was I going to be carried over this in safety?

A moment later, and, giddy and confused, I found myself not only over, but brought to a dead stop by Rawdon, who, quivering all over with excitement, had brought me right to the finish; only three other gentlemen were there besides the master of the hounds. I felt in an extremely awkward position. One of them, Sir Charles Courtenay, I slightly knew, as he was a great friend of General Forsyth. When he recognised me, he came forward at once.

'Miss Thorn, I congratulate you. This is the first meet of the season, and we have had the most splendid run, though a long one. Have you ever received a brush before?'

'It is all a mistake my being here,' I said with a little laugh, as I realized the humorous side of the situation. 'I am not one of your number; I was taking a quiet ride on the moor with a friend, when my horse, an old hunter, bolted with me, and has carried me here over every obstacle, in spite of my wishes.'

'It is a good horse, but a good rider too,' said the old gentleman. 'Very few ladies would have taken that last leap. Let me introduce the master of the hounds to you.'

The introduction took place, and, in spite of my protestations, the brush was presented, and then, one by one, other riders came upon the scene. It was a great relief to me when, turning my horse round, I came face to face with Kenneth.

'Goody Two-Shoes! What on earth are you doing here? Was it you, then, that took the lead so? We couldn't imagine what lady it was! I think I must be dreaming.' And Kenneth really looked as if he could not believe his eyes.

I explained it all hastily, adding, 'Do ride back with me away from all these people to meet Miss Rayner. She will be anxious about me.'

But Kenneth only shook his head with mock solemnity. 'Oh! Goody, Goody, I'm afraid you are a sad humbug! You won't make everybody believe that patched-up story. You didn't bargain for meeting me here. No wonder you don't want to come back to us just yet! I must write and tell the girls you are enjoying yourself in the hunting-field. Do you know that it is one of the governor's fads that girls are out of place in a hunt? Nell has always been refused permission to come with me. It will be amusing when this gets to the governor's ears!

Coming off by yourself on the sly, and getting the brush!'

And Kenneth gave a delighted chuckle at the end of his speech.

I rode straight away from him without a word, feeling ready to cry with vexation. Then, to my great delight, Miss Rayner rode up. Her eyes were twinkling with suppressed mirth.

'My dear girl, I am afraid Rawdon has given you a fright. I watched you over the gate and hedge; you took them well. I almost wished to be in your place, though my hunting days are over. I am proud of Rawdon!'

'I want to get away, Miss Rayner,' I said imploringly.

She looked at me, and was about to speak, when a gentleman rode up to her. 'Miss Rayner, I haven't seen you for years. I am glad to meet you in the field again.'

'Like this young lady who is staying with me, I have come into it accidentally. We were out riding, when her horse bolted with her, and I have only just come upon the scene. I have given up hunting for many years now. Let me introduce you, Miss Thorn; this is Colonel Hawkes, an old friend.'

For some minutes he and Miss Rayner carried on an animated conversation with one another. They seemed to have known each other in the past very intimately.

Presently Miss Rayner asked,—

'And where are you staying now?'

He hesitated; then said, slowly, 'With Ratcliffe—Charlie Ratcliffe. You remember him?'

Miss Rayner turned white to her lips; then said, in a cold, hard voice, 'I thought he was in the wilds of Africa?'

'He returned the end of last year. He finished the piece of work out there so satisfactorily for the Government that they want to send him out to another part, but he has refused. He says he wants to settle down quietly now, and has just bought a house somewhere in Surrey. He is a good fellow, but odd, you know. Since his return he has been slumming in the East End of London like a parson. I am staying with him at his chambers in town. We are such very old chums that I put up with his religious crotchets. He doesn't force them down one's throat, that's one comfort, and, I'm bound to admit, he lives them out.'

Miss Rayner changed the subject, and a few minutes after we rode away, very silent both of us, and we hardly exchanged a word till we reached home. All the evening Miss Rayner was very subdued and unlike herself. Susan had very truly described her to me as 'a fresh breeze coming in and out.' From the minute she set foot in a place, you were conscious of her cheery presence. Sometimes whistling to her dogs, chatting briskly to any in her path, and always full of energy and spirit; but now she sat with a dreamy, absent look in her eyes, and started if I addressed her on any topic. Later in the evening, as we sat over the drawing-room fire with our books, she suddenly looked up and said, 'Play to me, child; I am out of sorts. Colonel Hawkes brought up old scenes and memories which are best forgotten. Your music has always a soothing effect on me.'

I took my violin up, and leaning against the mantle-piece opposite to her, I began to play in the firelight. I played, as I loved to play, without notes before me, and soon I was in a dream myself. My favourite verse running through my head, I sought to bring it out of my violin, and as the last note died away I became conscious that Miss Rayner's eyes were glistening with tears. Knowing how utterly devoid of sentiment she generally seemed, I was the more surprised, only, of course, did not let her see I had noticed it.

'You have never played that before,' she said brusquely, as she recovered her composure.

'And I don't know that I could play it again,' I said. 'I never get it just the same. I was trying to bring out a thought that I am very fond of.'

'And what thought is that?'

'Do you know a verse like this?

> "These surface troubles come and go,
> Like rufflings of the sea;
> The deeper depth is out of reach
> To all, my God, but Thee."

There are two words in Jeremiah that I try and take for my life's motto: "Dwell deep." I love to bring it out of my violin.'

Miss Rayner smiled. 'I should not have thought there had been much occasion in your life at present for you to put those words into practice.'

I was silent. No doubt my small troubles seemed very insignificant to her who had perhaps seen and gone through far heavier ones herself.

After a little, she said thoughtfully, as she gazed into the glowing coals before her, 'One sometimes wonders, if certain passages in our lives were given us again, whether we would act differently; but I am inclined to think as a rule we should not.' Then, turning to me abruptly, she said, 'Would you like to hear why I have never married? I am not ashamed of anything—there is no need why you should not know—only I do not care to discuss bygone tales too often; so I shall not expect you to refer to it again. I was engaged to Charles Ratcliffe for six years. He, Colonel Hawkes, and I were always together; we hunted, danced, and amused ourselves as the rest of the world. Charlie—Mr. Ratcliffe—was then a struggling young barrister, and we waited for more prosperous times. About a year before we were to have been married, he'—she paused and gave a hard little laugh, 'well —he got "converted," as you would express it. I tried to laugh him out of it at first, but it was of no use; he gradually withdrew from amusements, and tried to make me do the same. We pulled together a little while longer, and then I saw it wouldn't do, and I told him so. "How can two walk together, except they be agreed?" There is no truer verse than that in the Bible. And so we parted, and I have never seen him from that day to this.'

'I am so sorry!' I murmured, as she paused as abruptly as she commenced.

'Oh, I am not an object of pity, I assure you!' she said, laughing: 'it was odd running up against Colonel Hawkes to-day. Did you see Kenneth there, too? I fancied I saw him in the distance.'

'Yes,' I said, seeing she wished to turn to other subjects; 'I am afraid he will never let me forget it. I wish he were not such a tease. He would misunderstand me, or pretend to do so. I shall not hear the last of it for a long time, I know.'

Miss Rayner laughed. 'I suppose he could not understand seeing you acting such a different role from your usual one. Never mind, child. Words do not break bones. Let him have the enjoyment of it. Perhaps this afternoon's exploit may have given you a taste for the hunting-field? Is it so?'

I shook my head. 'No, I don't think I shall want to mount Rawdon again while I am here. I could never trust him.'

That night I could not sleep, or get Miss Rayner's story out of my head. She only gave me the bare facts, but I could supply much that was not told. I could see that all her likes and dislikes were strong ones. Her affection for him had been no light girlish fancy, but had deepened, I could not help thinking, since separation. I wondered if he still thought of her, and whether the blank had been as great in his life as in hers. But then I remembered that he had what she had not—a satisfied soul and an unseen personal Friend. I felt a great pity for her. I knew from what I had heard from others that she had withdrawn herself from society for many years, and rightly conjectured that when the one she really cared about was no longer to be met there, it failed to satisfy or amuse her. And I longed that even yet she might find the same Saviour as he had, and become satisfied in the same way. Earnestly did I pray that she might be led to seek for this, and that if it was God's will that earthly happiness should be denied her, she still might be filled with the joy and peace 'which passes understanding' from above.

CHAPTER XI

A DIFFERENT ATMOSPHERE

'And I should fear, but lo! amid the press,
The whirl and hum and pressure of my day,
I hear Thy garments sweep, Thy seamless dress,
And close beside my work and weariness
Discern Thy gracious form, not far away,
But very near,
O Lord, to help and bless.'

—*Susan Coolidge*

My visit to Miss Rayner now drew to a close. I was really
sorry to leave her, and I think she was sorry to part with me.
It was a strange friendship between us. She was far beyond
me in knowledge of the world and in intellect, and yet I
know she said things to me that she would not say to any one
else. She would laugh at me, tease me, and never spare my
blushes of embarrassment and discomfiture; but as she was
wishing me good-bye the last afternoon, she put both her
hands on my shoulders and stood looking down upon me
with a strange softening of face and manner. 'I have liked
having you here, child; I knew I should from the first
moment I saw you, and I shall miss you after you have gone.
But I do not mean to lose sight of you, and when you want

advice,—or shall I say comfort?—come over and take advantage of my quiet resting-place here to soothe and solace yourself. It is strange advice to give you, but though I may have chaffed you about your religious views, keep a firm grip of them, and go on your own way straight-forward, without bending or relaxing in the slightest. I believe you have got hold of the real thing, and if you have, I should think it was worth keeping.'

Tears were in my eyes, and I laid my hand on her arm. 'I am praying that you may find it too, Miss Rayner—or rather Him, for it is Christ Himself that fills my life.'

She stooped and kissed me, but did not say another word, only there was a wistful look in her eyes that haunted me for long afterwards. Old John had his say, too, when parting with me at the station: 'I hope you have h'enjoyed your visit, miss, and have had an h'edifying time; the mistress wants some one of her h'own sex to talk to h'on h'occasions, though, h'as I h'often say, she can hold her h'equal with h'any man if she chooses. H'and h'if I make bold to say so, h'if you want a mount h'at h'any time, Rawdon shall be h'at your disposal; you did him credit the h'other day with the hounds, h'and I shall never raise h'any h'objection to h'allowing you to ride him!'

It was certainly a different kind of life to which I returned. The house was full of visitors, and all chance of quiet seemed gone. I think Violet and Nelly were genuinely glad to see me. Kenneth, of course, did not spare me; he coloured the story so of the way I had joined the hounds, as to make General Forsyth quite vexed, and Mrs. Forsyth did not seem to believe my true version of it.

'Why do you love to make people uncomfortable if you can?' I said in desperation to him, after he had been chaffing me unmercifully on the same subject before a lot of people in the drawing-room one afternoon.

'Because it is my nature to, I suppose,' he retorted. 'I don't think anything would make you uncomfortable, Goody! You go serenely on your way, wrapped in a cloak of supreme self-content and satisfaction. Except for bringing a little extra pink colour into your cheeks, which I like to see, no words of mine can ever stir you.'

'I have feelings,' I said, 'though I do try not to show them. I am not a piece of stone. And if I did show them, you would be the first to blame me for it.'

'I dare say I should, for it would be highly inconsistent with the profession that you make to lose your temper like ordinary mortals.'

'So that I cannot act rightly in any case in your eyes,' I said, half laughing, half vexed. 'I am just good as a kind of target that you can fire off volleys of ridicule at: if I resent it, it will be showing anger; if I bear it, it will be because I am "wrapped in a cloak of supreme self-content and satisfaction."'

'Upon my word, Goody, I think you are showing too much feeling now,' was the laughing rejoinder; 'I think I must make myself scarce till you are calmer.' And he walked away and left me. He was the only one of the Forsyths that I did not quite understand. No one said unkinder things to my face than he did, and yet behind my back I knew that many a time he had made things smoother for me with his parents. He laughed and scoffed openly at the weaknesses and insincerity of society, yet mingled freely in it, and was a favourite wherever he went. I felt no eye in the household was so keen as his on my words and actions; he was always wanting me to do things for him and go to places with him; yet when I was with him he would be unsparing in his scoffing remarks on any subject that would touch me most deeply. I found it best to take all he said as quietly as possible, only now and then protesting, as I had done upon this afternoon.

Hugh's friend, a Mr. Stanton, arrived a week after my return. He was rather a grave-looking man, tall and broad-shouldered, with dark eyes which seemed quick to take in every one and everything, and yet which had a kindly gleam in them.

We did not see much of him, for Hugh and he spent most of their days in the study together; but he proved very entertaining in the evening, for he had travelled a great deal and could talk well, and somehow or other would raise the conversation to a higher level than usual. General Forsyth would discuss questions of the day with him, with a keener interest than was his custom with a younger man; and Nelly came gushingly to confide in me the first night of his arrival: 'I like him awfully, Hilda! He is so different to most of Hugh's friends. They seem so hard and cynical, and have such a contempt for women, I always fancy. Mr. Stanton takes as much trouble to talk to me as he does to father, and he is awfully good-looking!'

One evening, soon after he arrived, General and Mrs. Forsyth and Constance wore dining out. A Miss Willoughby and her brother were staying in the house; they were cousins of the Forsyths, and had returned from London with them, but I had always kept away from them, as Miss Willoughby's manner and ways grated on me. She seemed utterly devoid of all religion, and was always ready to scoff and jeer at serious subjects. She was a clever woman of the world, and looked upon me as a mere child.

As we were in the drawing-room together, before the

gentlemen joined us after dinner, she called to me from her seat by the fire, 'Come here, you little piece of innocence, I want to talk to you; why do you always creep into a remote corner of the room away from everybody? Is it modesty, or misanthropy, that drives you from your fellow-creatures?'

'Neither,' I said, as I slowly moved towards the fireplace and took a seat near her. 'Nelly was entertaining you, so you did not require me.'

'But I do want you. I think you could be far more entertaining than Nelly here, because you have taken up an original role, and I like originality.'

I made no reply. There was a mischievous light in her eyes which warned me she meant to enjoy herself at my expense.

She lay back in her chair, put up her pince-nez, and regarded me for some minutes in silence. Then she gave a mock sigh.

'I don't see the halo, Nelly; it ought to be there—round her head, you know. I hope she isn't a sham saint!'

'You shall not tease her,' Nelly said warmly; 'she gets quite enough of that from Kenneth without your taking it up.'

'My dear child, I have no intention of teasing her. I would not presume to do so on such short acquaintance. Beyond "Good-night" and "Good-morning," I don't believe Miss Thorn and I have exchanged half a dozen words. We are going to converse agreeably together now, if you will allow us.'

'I don't think we shall find that we have much in common, Miss Willoughby,' I said, trying to speak pleasantly.

Amy Le Feuvre

'I dare say not. I am a wicked sinner according to your standard, and you are a righteous saint; but may not sinners sometimes speak to saints? How else are they to be made better, "I want to know," as the Americans say? Do you attend chapel, Miss Thorn?'

'No,' I answered a little shortly.

'I went into a chapel once,' she pursued, looking gravely at me, 'and there was a revival going on, I was told. That is what led me in there—I wanted to see a revival! After the sermon was over, an old white-haired man came stumbling into the seat where I was, and sat down beside me. "Young pusson," he said, "do you want to be converted?" "What does it feel like?" I asked. He rose up, and stood swelling out his waistcoat visibly. "It feels as if earth can't contain yer at times, and 'even's only big enough for yer." "Thank you," I said; "I shouldn't care to feel that size. Earth is big enough for me at present," and I walked out.'

A burst of laughter from behind announced that the gentlemen had entered the room. Kenneth came up to us, and planted himself on the hearthrug in front of us.

'Are you treating Goody Two-Shoes to one of your stories?' he asked.

'We are having a very serious conversation,' said Miss Willoughby, in her clear, loud voice, 'and do not wish to be interrupted. Now, Miss Thorn, is your experience like that of the old chapel saint? I have always heard that the godly were very big in their own estimation, but never quite so big as that I How big do you feel? Tell us. I have a fancy, if I were to try to attain to it, that it would be the old fable of the toad and the ox again being enacted. What is your opinion?'

'It is not a subject for jesting,' I said gravely; and I rose from my seat to move away. She laughingly caught hold of both my hands and detained me.

'Now you are my prisoner, and I shall not let you escape till you have answered a few questions. I have been doing my best to become acquainted with you, but you listen and reply in monosyllables, which is most unsociable. You leave me to do all the talking, and I want to hear your side of the question. Is she always so silent, Kenneth?'

'Silence marks her displeasure,' Kenneth replied, laughing.

'I don't like sulky natures,' Miss Willoughby went on provokingly, without giving me time to speak. 'I don't think she is shy, and I have said nothing to displease her. My object has been to become friends with her, but I'm afraid she thinks me too unworthy of her friendship. Now, Miss Thorn,—what a baby face it is, to be sure!—look up and speak. You don't seem so glib on the subject as you ought to be. What is "conversion"? Enlighten us.'

I looked up at my tormentor. 'You will find the best definition of it in the dictionary, if you are anxious to know,' I said.

'That is evading my question. I begin to think you have a good deal of cowardice in your composition. You are afraid to show your colours. Now I am going to ask you a straightforward question, and I expect a straightforward reply. Are you converted?'

Hugh and Mr. Stanton at this juncture joined our group, and there was a sudden lull in the conversation. Miss Willoughby, without relinquishing her hold of me, turned towards them with a face brimful of fun.

Amy Le Feuvre

'It's a case being tried,' she said to them. 'I am cross-examining a witness.'

'A prisoner, I should say,' observed Hugh drily.

'I shall not run away, Miss Willoughby,' I said, trying to speak amicably.

She dropped my hands at once, and I hoped the subject would be changed; but such was not her intention.

'I am waiting for your answer,' she pursued. 'Are you converted?'

I held my head erect and looked her straight in the face. 'Yes, I am.'

'Good! When were you converted? No hesitation. You are bound in honour not to run away from me, and I have several more questions yet to ask.'

'About six months ago in London,' My tone was grave. I did not know how this was going to end.

'Describe the process.'

'That I refuse to do, Miss Willoughby.'

'Then I shall not believe in you, for I expect you can't do it. And it is a selfish, unkind spirit to refuse to enlighten an inquirer. My old chapel friend was far kinder. You good people say conversion is a blessing; yet, when I want to know how to get it, you refuse to assist me.'

'If you want to know the way, the Bible will show you,' I said in a low voice.

'The Bible! I heard a clergyman say once that the Bible did not teach conversion!'

'But our Lord did. "Except ye be converted, and become as little children, ye shall not enter into the kingdom of heaven."'

It was Mr. Stanton who spoke, and every one looked up astonished.

'Do you know all about these things, Mr. Stanton?' questioned Miss Willoughby, as she looked at him curiously.

'I am glad to say I do,' he replied, 'and shall be pleased at any time to have a quiet talk with you about them.'

She shrugged her shoulders with a comic look of dismay at Kenneth. 'He looks as if he could be aggressive—it's a revelation to me; I cannot get over it! Let us have some music to refresh us after such topics!'

She moved across to the piano, and left me in peace for the remainder of the evening.

CHAPTER XII

A TEST

'As woods, when shaken by the breeze,
Take deeper, firmer root;
As winter's frosts but make the trees
Abound in summer fruit;
So every bitter pang and throe
That Christian firmness tries,
But nerves us for our work below,
And forms us for the skies.'

—Henry Francis Lyte

It was not to be wondered at that my thoughts dwelt much upon Mr. Stanton for the next few days. It was so strange to feel that there was another now in the house who was a follower of Christ, and I wondered if he would have a good influence over Hugh.

One afternoon I was coming back from the village, where I had been to give Jim his reading lesson, when Mr. Stanton overtook me, and we walked home together. I had never as yet seen him alone, and felt a little shy of him; but he soon made me feel at ease by his ready sympathy, and I found myself telling him of my different interests in the village.

And then he presently said, 'Do you find your life difficult at times in such surroundings?'

'Sometimes I do,' I responded, 'but never too difficult.'

'No,' he said; 'we are never placed in circumstances where it is impossible to serve our Master. I sometimes wish a little more of the martial spirit could be instilled into many Christians. A true soldier does not shirk or shrink from the front in battle, but a Christian is very apt to hide his colours if he gets upon the enemy's ground.'

'It is a puzzle to me sometimes,' I said, 'when it is best to keep silent and when to speak. One's life ought to tell most amongst unconverted people, and yet that tempts one sometimes to hide one's light. It is easy to go on one's way quietly without saying a word to any one, but perhaps it is not being faithful. What do you think about it, Mr. Stanton?'

'I think,' he said, 'if we are living close to the Master, He will never leave us in doubt as to when the opportunity for speaking occurs. If we are ready and waiting on Him, we shall be led to do the right thing. Many good people do more harm than good by making up their minds that they are bound to deliver a message, whether the occasion warrants it or not. And then it is often done in their own strength, and not in the power of the Spirit. I think the answer to all such difficulties is: Live close to Christ, and let Him give you your orders—no one else. The longer I live, the more strongly I feel how useless it is to go by other Christians' experiences. God leads us all in different ways. Let us strive to learn the sound of His slightest whisper, and take His Word only as our guide. We cannot go wrong then.'

We talked on till we reached home. I could not help feeling the comfort of having some one to speak to on the subjects

Amy Le Feuvre

that were so dear to me. I had had so few to help or advise me, and though I knew the truth of what Mr. Stanton said, that we could not frame our lives by others' experiences, yet, as a young Christian, I felt refreshed and strengthened by his words. When I said something of this sort to him, he smiled.

'You have not suffered by the loneliness of your position, Miss Thorn; it has only brought you to know Christ more intimately, and to lean upon Him harder. I have seen a good deal of young Christians pinning their faith to a human being: in some cases a friend who has been the means of their conversion, or a favourite preacher. It is natural, but Satan often uses it as a snare. The Master is not appealed to so often as the friend. He sinks into the background, and when the friend is removed they feel utterly stranded, and in some cases fall back in their Christian life.'

When we reached the house, we found every one in the drawing-room at tea. Miss Willoughby was in high spirits. She was organizing some tableaux that the Forsyths were trying to get up, and was pressing every one into her service.

'Now, Hilda Thorn,' she said laughingly, as I entered the room, 'I am going to ask you a great favour. Don't purse up that little mouth of yours in anticipation. It is nothing sinful, upon my honour it is not.'

'You shall not torment her till she has had a cup of tea,' said Nelly good-naturedly. 'Come and sit down by me, Hilda.'

'Will you give her plenty of sugar then, please, Mrs. Forsyth?' Miss Willoughby pursued; 'I want her temper sweetened.'

'I don't think she possesses a temper,' put in Kenneth. 'I know for a fact that I often lose mine in trying to make her lose hers!'

'If she never loses it, she must have it in her possession,' said Miss Willoughby drily; and every one laughed.

'What is it you want?' I asked a few moments after, having disposed of my tea.

'Just at present we want a little soothing. There is an east wind to-day, and not being a piece of perfection like yourself, I feel on edge! I have not been treated well. I had my eye on Mr. Stanton for King Arthur, and Hugh tells me they are dining in town on the 6th, which is the date we have fixed. I suspect they have arranged it between them. Then Constance and I want to pose for the same character; she thinks she is better suited to it than I, and she likes her own way. I think the contrary, and I like mine. And the fact is that I've been told that you are a great violinist—"Music hath power to soothe the savage breast." Will you do us the favour of playing to us now? We shall feel more peaceably disposed towards each other afterwards, I know.'

I willingly complied, and played one thing after another. When I put down my violin, I saw Miss Willoughby give an approving nod towards Mrs. Forsyth, and then she said, 'Thank you—that is a great treat. Now I feel at peace with all mankind; do you?'

'I think I generally do,' I replied.

'Well, now, what I want to ask you is this,—and I am sure you will not be so ill-natured as to refuse,—would you mind playing a little like that just behind a screen for us? You won't be seen at all, and no one will know who it is. Nelly says you have scruples about taking part in tableaux; but of course this could not be an objection.'

Miss Willoughby dropped the half-mocking tone in which

Amy Le Feuvre

she usually addressed me, and for an instant I felt I could not refuse. Nelly saw my hesitation, and took advantage of it. 'Do say "Yes," Hilda; we want a violin, and Violet does play so atrociously; there is no one about here that can do it as well as you. It will only be for about ten minutes.'

'Why do you want it?' I asked.

'I will tell you,' said Kenneth; 'we are to have some moving tableaux, illustrating certain pithy sayings. Miss Willoughby has mentioned the one we want you for,—"Music hath charms," etc. I think I am to pose as one of the villains. We are divided as to whether it is to be a duel or a cold-blooded murder; but I know my part is to transform my face from that in which diabolical hatred and fiendish rage is depicted, into a gradual state of simpering, smiling imbecility, and I think the curtain will fall upon me and my rival locked in each other's arms, shedding maudlin tears of love into our respective shirt-fronts!'

'The moral is so awfully good,' urged Nelly; 'do be obliging just this once, Hilda.'

'Of course she is going to do it,' said Miss Willoughby.

'I will give you an answer to-morrow,' I said slowly, and taking up my hat and cloak I left the room.

It was hard sometimes to keep clear of the gaiety around me, and this was one of the cases in which I much wished for advice. I felt inclined to appeal to Mr. Stanton; he had stood a little apart from the others talking to General Forsyth, but I felt sure that he had been within earshot of the whole conversation. Yet his words that afternoon came back to me. I must get my orders from my Master, and not from him. And, as so often before, I went down on my knees in my room, and with my Bible before me sought the advice I needed.

I felt, when I at length rose, that I was best out of it altogether. I knew my wish to oblige them and show them that I had no ill-feeling about it might land me into further difficulties. It would be the thin end of the wedge. And though I dreaded the scoffing remarks of Miss Willoughby, and knew she would be really put out by my refusal, my mind was quite made up, and meeting her on the stairs going down to dinner two hours later, I told her I could not do it.

She only laughed at me. 'Nonsense, child! you will think better of it; don't be in such a hurry to refuse.' Then, drawing my arm within hers, she went on in a coaxing tone as we descended the stairs together: 'I have taken a liking to you, Hilda, for I feel you have a true ring about you. I am afraid I am a dreadful tease, but I tell you honestly I admire and respect your religious views. Much better be one thing or the other—and there is no uncertain sound about you. But don't you think it a pity in the present instance if, in your mistaken zeal, you would lose the opportunity of rendering us a little service, and so commending your religion practically to us? I was talking to a gentleman the other day who said, "What I object to so much in these so-called good people is their extreme selfishness and indifference to the likes and dislikes of those with whom they live; good nature and the ordinary common little courtesies of life seem altogether lacking in their composition." This isn't much we are asking of you, and I don't think you will refuse. Five minutes only we want from you. You needn't be present at the tableaux at all; people will think it is some hired musician in the background, and you can escape to your room immediately afterwards. If you refuse, do you think it will bring credit on your religion? It's the only favour I have ever asked of you, and it is such a little kindness to do.'

Amy Le Feuvre

It was hard, in the face of this, to adhere to my resolve. If I had not come straight from prayer, I don't believe I could have withstood her.

'I am afraid you will think me very disagreeable,' I said as gently as I could; 'but I have thought over it, and have made up my mind that it is best for me not to take part in the tableaux at all. I think with a little practice Violet will do what you require.'

Miss Willoughby's face was not a pleasant one to see when she saw I really was in earnest. She dropped my arm at once, and seeing Kenneth hovering about in the hall she went up to him, 'Take me out into the balcony; I want a change of atmosphere. Your converted people are all alike. A nasty, spiteful, ill-natured set of canting hypocrites!'

'It's war to the knife between you two now,' whispered Kenneth to me as we went in to dinner; 'and I warn you she will give you no quarter. She is not accustomed to have her plans thwarted. You had better give in!'

I wondered why Miss Willoughby should have set her heart so upon my helping them; but that night, when I went to bed, I was enlightened.

Miss Graham tapped at my door, and asked if she might come in for a few minutes. She very often had a firelight talk with me at bedtime. I was not feeling inclined for it now, for Miss Willoughby, though purposely ignoring me in the drawing-room after dinner, had been lavish with her biting sarcasm on Christianity and some of its followers.

Mr. Stanton had instantly come forward, upon hearing some of her remarks, and in the discussion that followed she had been decidedly worsted. Mr. Stanton was not a man to be trifled with, and he told her some very plain truths. From getting excited, she finally lost her temper, and the evening had ended unpleasantly for us all. I felt I had been the innocent cause of it, and was too much perturbed in spirit to relish a long chat with Miss Graham.

She surprised me by alluding at once to the subject of my thoughts. 'Have you consented to play for them at the tableaux?'

'No,' I said a little wearily as I sat down, and drew a chair forward for her. 'I have told Miss Willoughby I cannot do it.'

'Is that your final decision? Does she know it is?'

'Yes, and she is very vexed about it.'

'Of course she is. My dear Hilda, I am glad. I think I must tell you now about it. She is a clever woman, but not a good one. Do you know that it has been a regular trap for you? Governesses are not supposed to have ears—and yesterday I was giving Violet a music lesson, when she and Mr. Kenneth and Miss Forsyth came in. They went over to the window seat, and there began talking over these tableaux. They did not lower their voices, and she made a bet with Mr. Kenneth that she would make you take part in them. He laughed at her, but she said she was in earnest, and then when he had left the room she propounded her plan to Constance. If you had agreed to play for them,—which she said she was pretty sure she would make you do,—she was going to arrange that just before the curtain fell the screen should be suddenly shifted from in front of you, and you would then be in full view of the audience. You were, in fact, to personify the girl for whom the two rivals were fighting.'

'But,' I said, quite bewildered, 'I should not have been

Amy Le Feuvre

dressed for the occasion. How could she imagine such a plan would succeed?'

'It was all to be arranged. She said your cream silk would be just the thing, and Mr. Forsyth was to tell you to wear it that night for dinner. I assure you Miss Willoughby was quite determined that she should succeed. I am very glad she has failed, for it would be a shabby trick to play any one, and I was very vexed that it should be played on you.'

I was silent. Miss Graham's words were a revelation to me, and I wondered what I had done to cause Miss Willoughby to act so. And I understood her anger at having had her plans so frustrated. How thankful I was that I had not yielded to her entreaties! After a pause, Miss Graham said, 'You must have a wonderful grip of unseen things, Hilda, to live your life here so cheerily and brightly, when you have such constant difficulties and disagreeables arising between you and the girls.'

I looked up at her. 'It is a happy life, Miss Graham, and no circumstances can ever make it otherwise.'

She leant forward in the firelight, and, taking one of my hands in hers, said rather brokenly, with tears glistening in her eyes,—

'I have wanted to tell you—I must to-night; I think it will cheer you to know that I have found what you have. Do you remember those few words you said to me in the wood soon after you first came? I could never forget them. And I was troubled for long afterwards. But I see it all so differently now; salvation is not to be earned, as you said to me, but to be received. And I think when one receives salvation, one receives the Giver with it. I know I have found it so—it does indeed make life different.'

'Oh, Miss Graham, I am so glad!' I said, and, unable to check myself, I burst into tears. I think I was overwrought, and this coming on the top of my other trouble, proved too much for me.

'How long have you—have you known this?' I asked, and in the fulness of my heart I leant over and kissed her.

'I don't know,' she said with a smile; 'I have been seeking for it on my knees and with my Bible night after night. Sometimes I fancied I had the assurance of it, and then it seemed to leave me. I think when you were at Miss Rayner's I seemed to doubt less and trust more. And now I don't think I have a doubt at all. I am staking my assurance on verses like John vi. 37. It was seeing you live your life here that showed me you must have the real thing, and made me long to have it too.'

She left me soon after, and I sat on by my fire with silent thanks in my heart for this news. God had indeed been good to me, and I felt especially grateful that I had been sent such comfort and cheer after a rather trying evening.

Amy Le Feuvre

CHAPTER XIII

TAKEN HOME

'But I like to think of him passing,
Like a clear early star,
Into that quiet region …
I like to think of his little feet
Climbing the heavenly stair,
Of his eyes in their wondering meekness
Waking to glory there.'

The next morning I was out in the garden picking a few late chrysanthemums, when Mr. Stanton passed by me. He stopped for a moment.

'What answer have you given about the tableaux?' he asked, with a smile.

'I have declined to play,' I said. 'I told Miss Willoughby so yesterday evening before dinner.'

He looked away thoughtfully into the distance, and then said quietly, 'That accounted for her vexation last night. I wondered why she was so bitter. Poor girl! one feels sorry for a life like that.' Then looking at me rather intently, he asked, 'Is the violin consecrated to God, Miss Thorn?'

'I don't know,' I stammered; 'I hope so, but I don't keep it for sacred music only. I play to them when they want me to. Is that wrong? Surely not! And I love it so myself; it seems to raise my thoughts heavenwards. Do you think I ought to play nothing but hymns on it?'

He laughed. 'No, I do not; and if I did, you ought not to take my words as a leading to you. For myself, I believe that music is a gift entrusted to us by our Father, and if we give innocent pleasure to others by our talent we are not using it in vain. Only I think you were wise in keeping clear of the tableaux. If you mingle in one thing, you must in another, and a Christian has to walk very carefully if he wishes to preserve unbroken communion with his God.'

He said no more, and left me. As I came into our morning room a little time after, I heard Miss Willoughby's animated voice,—

'I should like to clear them both out of the house. He is the least objectionable, as he can be entertaining when he chooses, but I can't imagine why she should take up her abode here. It is not a question of charity.' Here she noticed my entrance, but calmly went on talking to Constance as if I were not there. 'Let her take herself off to some nursing Sisterhood or slum work in the East of London. I hate a half-and-half kind of person. If they are too good to live our life and mingle in our society, let them take up a religious vocation, instead of being a perpetual source of annoyance and aggravation to those they are with.'

Constance gave a slight laugh, then changed the conversation. I put my flowers in water, then left the room without a word. I found Kenneth's words very true. Miss Willoughby could not forgive me, and I was constantly reminded of her dislike to my presence. Constance sided

Amy Le Feuvre

with her; she had never liked me, and Nelly, though now and then warm in my defence, seemed to be a little afraid of disagreeing with her, and rather kept out of my way when her cousin was near. It was trying to bear and her words now set me thinking, as I had sometimes thought before. Should I be wiser to leave the Forsyths, and go into work of some sort that would be more congenial? If my presence in the house was a trial to them, why should I not relieve them of it? And yet at present I hardly saw the way plain before me. 'Dwell deep,' I said to myself. 'Miss Willoughby will not be here always, and I have had the cheer of Miss Graham. I have much to be thankful for.'

It was indeed a comfort to me to be able to talk over things with Miss Graham. We began having a little Bible reading and prayer together at night, and it refreshed and strengthened us both. She seemed to have taken such a firm hold of the truth, and to have such a freshness in her enjoyment of her Bible, that it did me good to hear her talk. Now and then, too, I enjoyed a few words with Mr. Stanton, but not very often. He and Hugh were much up in town, and he was very busy writing some scientific book in which Hugh was helping. Once Hugh had asked me to go in and play on my violin to them in the dusk before dinner; but Mrs. Forsyth had told me afterwards she would rather I did not do it again, and I took care not to repeat it. I was left very much to myself while the preparations for the tableaux were going on, and when the night came I found that Mrs. Forsyth had no objection to my having a schoolroom tea with Violet and Miss Graham, and so keeping out of the way of it all. Violet was allowed in to see them, but Miss Graham did not care to go, and she and I spent a very pleasant evening together. Miss Willoughby and her brother left a few days after; but up to the last day she was unsparing in her comments and gibes on everything serious. She was ridiculing me on the morning of the day she left, when we were gathered round the drawing-room fire just before luncheon. I could not well make my escape, so bore it as quietly as I could; but to my surprise Kenneth turned upon her. 'Now look here, Florence,' he said, 'you have had it all your own way since Goody made you lose your bet; don't you think you can part from her in peace? She has stood your fire well. I like to see fair play, and I think you have had your innings. Upon my word, I give her a good dose on occasions, just to keep her from getting too uppish and trying to ride it with a high hand over us; but you beat me altogether!'

Miss Willoughby laughed a little scornfully, but she took the hint, and when she said good-bye her better nature overcame her.

'Well, we will part as friends, Miss Thorn. Your face is the best part of you; your views are odious, but no doubt you mean well. I bear no malice; do you?'

'No,' I said, looking up at her gravely; 'but I do wish you understood my motives better.'

She laughed and turned away, and so we parted.

I found everything easier after her departure.

One evening we were just going in to dinner, when one of the servants came up to me. 'If you please, miss, a message has come from the village that Jim Carter is ill, and wants to see you at once.'

I knew the boy had been poorly, for two days before I had found him in bed with a bad sore throat, and we had had to postpone the reading lesson. His uncle said it was a cold, but I had thought then it was a severe one. I turned to ask Mrs. Forsyth if she would excuse my coming in to dinner, but she would not hear of this.

'It is great impertinence to send up at our dinner hour with such a request. I cannot agree to your running down to the village as late as this. The boy must wait till to-morrow.'

'Oh, let me just run down after dinner, then!' I pleaded. 'I am afraid he must really be very ill.'

'What is the matter with him? If it is anything infectious, you must not go near him.'

'I think it is a bad cold.'

'Come in to dinner at once. We cannot keep every one waiting.'

I obeyed, but was very silent through the meal. My thoughts were with Jim, and I longed to be with him. Hugh, who was sitting next me, asked why I was so grave. When I told him, he said, 'I am going out for a smoke after dinner, so I will take you if you like. The mother won't have any objection then, I fancy.'

I thanked him, and Mrs. Forsyth giving her consent, an hour later we left the house together. As we were walking down the lane, Hugh said abruptly, 'How do you like Stanton?'

'Very much,' I said; 'is he going to stay much longer?'

'I have just persuaded him to stay over Christmas. He has no belongings of his own, and I fancy finds his country house rather dreary.'

'I wonder he doesn't marry.'

Hugh looked at me rather curiously, then said, 'He is too particular. You good people are hard to please!'

'Have you known him long?'

'No, I was introduced to him last spring in town; but we have seen a good bit of each other since. He is one of the few I know who reconcile science and religion together. And I will acknowledge he has made me change some of my opinions about those matters. He is rather a big man in the literary world.'

'I am always thankful when clever men are true Christians,' I said; 'so many people think that the two can never co-exist.'

When we reached Jim's home, Hugh said he would wait outside for me. I found old Roger sitting by the boy's bed, with real trouble in his face. Jim himself lay back almost motionless, except for a slight movement of his lips. At the bottom of his small bed little Roddy was perched, his round eyes looking full of interest and curiosity, and Roddy's mother was bustling about, every now and then putting her apron to her eyes.

I bent over Jim, and called him by name. He opened his eyes, and smiled feebly; then I caught the murmured words, 'Read me about the city.'

'He's very ill,' whispered old Roger to me; 'an' we can't get no doctor—but we've sent for 'un now. I thought I could a doctored him myself; but it's no good. He's 'ad no food for four-and-twenty hours.'

'It's inflammation of the throat or windpipe, I think,' put in Roddy's mother. 'I only knew he was so bad to-day, or I'd have been up sooner.'

Amy Le Feuvre

The sick boy's eyes looked at me wistfully, and again I caught the words, 'The city—I think I'm going there.' I turned to my little Bible, which I had brought with me, and read a few verses from the seventh and two last chapters in Revelation. His eyes brightened; he repeated slowly and with great difficulty, 'Washed—made white in the blood of the Lamb.'

'Yes,' I said gently, as I laid my hand on his fevered brow; 'and you have been washed, have you not, Jim?'

He nodded; and here little Roddy burst forth eagerly, 'Is Jim goin' to heaven?'

'We don't know,' I said; 'but he is quite ready to go if Jesus wants him.'

'What time will he get there?' demanded Roddy. 'Will he get there to-morrow day?'

His mother hushed him, and then old Roger asked me to pray with them, which I did as simply as I could, for I saw Jim's eyes following my every movement, and knew he was quite conscious.

'I think I will take Roddy home to bed, and step up again,' said Mrs. Walters, 'if you're so good as to stay here with the old man, miss. The doctor won't be long now, I'm thinkin'.'

Roddy stoutly resisted being taken away at first.

'I wants to see Jim go. I wants to see the angels come for him!'

When he was finally pacified, and about to be led away, he trotted up to Jim, and putting his rosy mouth against his cheek, said in a loud whisper, 'I sends my love to Jesus, Jim. Will you 'member?'

And when Jim smiled and nodded, he departed with his mother, looking back with a shining face to say,—

'Good-bye, Jim. You send me a post letter when you get to heaven, like uncle does to mother!'

I sat on quietly for a little while, with Jim's hot hand clasped in mine, repeating some verses to him, and then the doctor arrived, and Hugh put his head in rather impatiently at the door. Jim would not leave go of my hand at first, but the doctor rather roughly put me aside.

'Never bend over a sick person so,' he said to me; 'especially if it's a case of a bad throat.'

I went to the door to Hugh. 'I am so sorry,' I said, 'but I promised Mrs. Walters to stay till she returned, and I should like to hear what the doctor says. Would you mind waiting a short time longer?'

He grumbled a little, but allowed me ten minutes more. The doctor did not stay very long, and then he came to me with a grave face. 'There is nothing to be done for him now,' he said; 'it is too late. I don't want to alarm you, but it is diphtheria. If I had been called in earlier, I might have saved him. You had better not stay. I doubt if the poor lad will last through the night. Is there any one besides this old man?'

'A neighbour is coming back directly,' I answered, my heart sinking within me at the tidings. 'You will just let me wish him good-bye?'

'If you have been with him much already it will not matter.

Amy Le Feuvre

Not too close to him, please.'

I stood at the bottom of the bed, and Jim's eyes at once sought mine questioningly.

I tried to smile. 'I mustn't stay, Jim; you are in the arms of Jesus, remember. Good-bye.'

His lips moved, but I could catch no sound; only a faint smile crossed his face, and I turned to the door to hide the tears already springing to my eyes. I had seen a great deal of Jim lately, and our reading lessons had drawn us very close together. He seemed to have grasped the truth as a little child, and I had no fears about his being one of the Lord's flock. Mrs. Walters entered the house directly after I had left Jim. She was very concerned when she learnt what it was, and anxious about Roddy, but promised to stay all night. One word I had with old Roger before I left.

'Ah!' he said, with a shake of his head, in response to the bit of comfort I tried to give him; 'I might a known the boy would be taken. He has been gettin' so fond of spellin' out of my big Bible lately, and mostly his talk has been of heaven, and the beautiful city, as he calls it. Well, the Lord wants him, and I'm not the one to say naught against the Lord's dealin's. He's allays merciful, the Lord is, and maybe my time will be comin' soon.'

When I joined Hugh outside I found Mr. Stanton with him. He told me Mrs. Forsyth was getting anxious at my long stay, and wished me to return immediately. He had volunteered to come down with the message.

I told them a little about Jim, but my heart was too full to say much, and we walked home very silently.

Just as we were reaching the hall door, Hugh happened to ask what was the matter with him, and when I told him, both he and Mr. Stanton looked much concerned.

Mrs. Forsyth was really angry when she knew.

'I wish I had prevented your going altogether. I can't conceive what made you stay such a time with him; it was most inconsiderate of you. I wish you had never taken up with these village boys; it is a constant anxiety to me that you may bring back infectious diseases from their homes.'

I told her how it was I had stayed so long, and then asked to be excused coming into the drawing-room that evening. I wanted to be alone; it had all seemed so sudden and unexpected that I could hardly realize it.

Early the next morning the village church bell began to toll, and I knew that my eldest scholar had gone home. It was a real grief to me, and yet for his sake I could not regret it. How thankful I was now that I had taken him into my Sunday class, in spite of his age! It seemed as if it was a special bit of work that God Himself had given me, and I thanked Him for it on my knees in the midst of my tears. I heard afterwards that he had not spoken to any one afterwards, or taken the slightest notice of anything, but had passed peacefully away about four o'clock in the morning.

Roddy remarked cheerfully, when he heard it, 'Jim will be glad now, won't he, mother? I wish the angels would come for me, too!'

CHAPTER XIV

WOOED AND WON

'Beloved! let us love so well, our work shall still be better
for our love,
And still our love be sweeter for our work;
And both commended for the sake of each,
By all true workers, and true lovers born.'

—E. B. Browning

It seemed as if Roddy's wish might be realized, for two days
after he sickened with the same complaint. Mrs. Forsyth
would not hear of my going near him, and I had to be content
with news from time to time through the different villagers. I
was not anxious about myself, but I did not feel well, and
when my throat began to pain me I felt pretty sure that I was
going to have it, too.

I was meditating whether I should tell Mrs. Forsyth one
afternoon, as I sat by the morning-room fire, when Nelly and
Kenneth came in from a walk glowing with health and
spirits.

'Now,' said Kenneth, throwing himself full length on the
sofa, 'we are very tired, and want a rest. Get your fiddle and

play to us in the gloaming, Goody!'

I did not feel much in the mood for it, but I thought it would take off my thoughts from myself, so I began to play. And in the firelight, with the flickering shadows over the room, I lost all sense of my audience. I seemed to see the golden gates of the Beautiful City, and Jim beckoning to both Roddy and myself. 'The Lamb which is in the midst of the throne shall feed them, and shall lead them unto living fountains of waters, and God shall wipe away all tears from their eyes.' These words came to me with a fresh realization of their beauty.

When I stopped playing, Nelly was regarding me with round open eyes, and Kenneth took me quite aback by saying, with cool deliberation, 'There are moments, Goody Two-Shoes, when you and your fiddle are before my eyes, that I think I should like to marry you and take you away with me somewhere where you should charm me with those strains continually. Don't look so frightened. We understand each other. I know you wouldn't dream of having me, so I am never going to ask you. You have certainly a fit of inspiration on you to-night. I don't think I have ever heard you play better.'

'Miss Thorn has tired herself I think,' said a voice near the door; and looking round, I saw that Mr. Stanton had been an unseen listener.

I sat down in my chair by the fire. 'I am tired,' I said. 'I think I shall go to bed, Nelly.'

Instantly Mr. Stanton came forward and gave me his arm. 'You are trembling all over,' he said very gently; 'lean on me. I am afraid it is your throat.'

I looked up at him. 'Yes,' I said. 'Will you ask Mrs. Forsyth to come to me? I am so sorry to give her the anxiety, but I am afraid I am going to be ill.'

There was a strange look in his eyes as his glance met mine —a look that haunted me through hours of weariness and pain afterwards. It seemed so full of tender concern and anxiety; but all he said was in a low tone as we left the room together, 'The eternal God is thy refuge, and underneath are the everlasting arms.'

Nelly came with me to my room, and in a very few moments her mother followed. I feared what Mrs. Forsyth might say, and began half apologising for the trouble I might give her; but she cut me short, and nothing could have been kinder or more restful than her words. She told Nelly to leave the room, helped me to bed herself, saying, 'Don't talk or worry yourself, child. I have sent for the doctor. It may be a very slight attack, and the quieter you keep the better. There is nothing for you to be anxious about. I shall send my maid to you presently; she is very good in sickness. Now lie still, and don't talk to any one. I only wish you had told me you were not feeling well before.'

The next week or ten days seemed like a dream; I hardly knew how ill I was till afterwards; but they had feared at one time that I would not pull through. The verse that Mr. Stanton gave me kept running through my head as a continual refrain: 'Underneath are the everlasting arms.' And I found it a wonderful pillow to rest upon. As I gradually recovered my health and strength, I was astonished at the extreme kindness of all in the house. My room was supplied with fresh flowers every day, and all varieties of books and magazines were constantly making their appearance.

Mrs. Forsyth was in and out of my room the whole time,

though she would not allow her daughters to come near me, and nothing could have exceeded her kindness and attention.

'How is Roddy?' was one of the first questions I asked.

Lyle, Mrs. Forsyth's maid, answered me. 'He is getting well, miss. His mother has been in a sore state of fright about him, but the doctor was hopeful about him from the first.'

When Christmas Day came, it found me still in my room; but on New Year's Day I made my first appearance downstairs. I was surprised to find how weak I felt, and was glad to rest on the couch which Kenneth wheeled up towards the fire in the drawing-room for me.

'We have missed you very much,' said Kenneth, with a twinkle in his eye that invariably came there when he spoke to me; 'I fell to quarrelling with Nell from lack of occupation; she doesn't stand fire like you! Haven't you missed me? I am sure you must have.'

'I don't think I have thought of you once,' I replied with truth.

'And who do you think sent you those beautiful flowers every day if I did not?'

'I don't think it was you,' I said decidedly.

He laughed, and Nelly put in, 'Of course he didn't. Mr. Stanton was constantly bringing some back from London, if he failed to coax old Brown to cut him some from the houses. I think he has been the most attentive one all through!'

'Of course he has. I think he was longing to go in and read the Bible to you, if the mother had let him. Ministration of

Amy Le Feuvre

the sick, don't you call it? He will be very attentive yet, I assure you. We know the way the wind lies, don't we, Nell?'

'I know this, that you are not going to bully Hilda the very first day she comes down.'

Kenneth turned away with his low chuckle, and Nelly came up, and sitting down by me, put her hand on mine caressingly. 'You look as white and fragile as a piece of china, Hilda. I am so glad you are better. You don't know how we have missed you, and when I thought we were going to lose you altogether I was miserable. I thought over all the nasty things we had said to you, and how you had borne it like an angel, and then I thought you were going to be taken away because you were too good for us, and I was wretched!'

Her eyes were full of tears. She added impulsively, 'I prayed that you might be spared to us. I promised God I would turn over a new leaf and be more serious, and I want to keep that promise. You will help me, will you not? I so often wish I was more like you!'

'Dear Nelly,' I said, tears coming to my own eyes, 'I will do what I can to help you. I know you will never regret it if you do keep that promise!'

More we could not say then, for others came up, Mr. Stanton amongst them. He smiled as he took my hand. 'Welcome back, Miss Thorn. Are you glad to be amongst us again?'

'Yes,' I said, looking up at him, 'I think I am, though at one time I thought I should like to go. I did not think I would be missed.'

He did not answer for a minute, then he said in a low voice, 'I think the Lord has more work for you to do yet in this corner of His vineyard.'

I thought of Nelly, and wondered if that was to be my work. How often I had prayed that she might have the desire given to her to be different! She had always appeared so perfectly content with her life, that I wondered if anything would ever convince her of its emptiness.

I saw a great deal of Mr. Stanton during my convalescence; he would sometimes come into the morning-room where Nelly and I spent most of our time, and bring me a book or paper to read, often sitting down and reading it himself to us. And I soon lost all sense of constraint with him, and could talk to him as unrestrainedly as I could to any one.

Miss Graham would often join us in her spare time, and the days passed so pleasantly that I dreaded a change in them.

One afternoon I was lying back in an easy chair by the fire alone, when Mr. Stanton came in.

'I thought I would enjoy a little chat with you before dinner,' he said. 'I am going away in two days' time, so may not have another opportunity.'

My heart sank within me, but I knew that it must come, and steadied my voice as I replied simply, 'I am sorry.'

'Are you?' he said, bending down over me with a look in his eyes that I could not meet. 'Will you miss me when I am gone? I have such a longing to stay and surround you with the love and tenderness that I feel for you—to have the right of protecting and shielding you from so many things that must distress you in your life here. I wonder what your feelings are towards me? Could you trust me with your dear little self, or am I too old, and too grave to suit you? Do you care for me just a little—Hilda?'

I could not answer. Somehow or other I had never expected this or looked for it. To have him as a friend was as much as I had ever hoped, and I felt confused and bewildered by the thoughts of anything more.

He seemed to read my thoughts. 'I have taken you by surprise; do not give me your answer now. I will wait till to-morrow. I think I could make you happy, my child,' and there was a little wistfulness in his tone. 'I know how happy you would make me.'

I tried to speak, but could not. He stood up by the fireplace, looking down at me silently for a moment, then said, 'Do not distress yourself; it is no light thing I am asking you—to give yourself away for life to one you know so comparatively little. If I were a younger man, I should not hesitate so. But I do think we have a bond together which many have not—that of being fellow-workers and servants of the same Master. And,' here his voice broke a little, 'Hilda, dear child, you have my love; shall I be able to win yours?'

Then, as I was still silent, he made a movement as if about to leave me. 'I will not press you—give me an answer to-morrow.'

But by this time I knew my own heart. I raised ply head and put my hand on his arm. 'Don't go,' I murmured; 'I will give you the answer now.'

And the answer never got put into words, for with his strong arm round me all doubts vanished, and I knew that no one on earth occupied such a position in my heart as he did.

'I don't know what General Forsyth will say,' I said, a little time after, when I heard the first gong sound for dinner.

'I had his permission to come to you,' was the reply.

I went into Mrs. Forsyth's boudoir before dinner, but she seemed to know all about it, and kissed me in a most motherly fashion. 'I can see what you have come to tell me, child, and you have the best wishes of both the general and myself. You are exactly suited to each other in all your peculiar views, and he is able to give you a comfortable home. I thought when you were first taken ill how it would end, he was so concerned about you!'

It certainly was a surprise to me that all in the house seemed to have expected it but myself.

'It stands to reason, my dear Goody,' observed Kenneth when he heard it, '"that birds of a feather flock together." I think myself he has the best of the bargain. That is the first compliment I have ever paid you, I believe!'

I seemed to live in a dream for the next few days, for Mr. Stanton—or Philip, as I soon learnt to call him—postponed his departure for a week. He took me out for drives on warm, bright days, and was continually with me. It seemed to change my whole life, and I could only thank God again and again for His goodness. I suppose I had been so accustomed to live my life alone without receiving sympathy or help from any, that I had ceased to expect it, and Philip's tender, watchful care over me seemed sometimes more than I could bear.

I broke down one afternoon altogether, and it was only some trifling little piece of attention on his part that did it. 'You spoil me,' I cried; 'I have never had any one to care for my likes or dislikes before. You will make me selfish, Philip.

Amy Le Feuvre

Don't be so good to me.'

'I shall not spoil you,' he responded, with a smile. 'I want to make your life brighter. You have had plenty of loneliness in it, and now I have the pleasure of altering all that. Dear child, a little love and care will not make you selfish.'

CHAPTER XV

A GATHERING CLOUD

'O friend! O best of friends! Thy absence more
Than the impending night darkens the landscape o'er!'

—Longfellow

'Miss Rayner is in the drawing-room, and would like to see you, miss,' was the message brought to me one afternoon.

I hastened in. She had been to see me twice whilst I was ill, but neither time was I well enough to enjoy her visit. I had written to tell her of my engagement, and was a little doubtful as to how she would receive the news. I had not heard from her since.

'Well,' she said, drawing me towards her by both hands, 'you haven't been long about this affair, child! You did not know such a person was in existence a couple of months ago. And it isn't a curate, after all!'

'Would you rather it had been, Miss Rayner?' I asked, laughing.

'I abominate the tribe, as you know, but, as far as I am

Amy Le Feuvre

concerned, this Mr. Stanton may not be much better. Who is he, and what is he? He is an unknown quantity to me!'

'He is a Christian and a gentleman,' I said warmly 'and one of Hugh's literary friends.'

'A dreamy book-worm like Hugh? That does not commend him to me; I should wish you something better. Now don't try to crush me with that fiery look. How do I know what he is like? I only know that you must have had very short acquaintance with him, and you could afford to wait. You are quite a child still.'

'Shall I call him and introduce him to you? He is in the house,' I asked very quietly, for I knew Miss Rayner was only trying to draw me out.

'Not just yet; my call is on you this afternoon. Are you feeling strong again? How that attack has pulled you down! Are they feeding you up well?'

'Yes, I am getting well fast.'

She sat down and talked to me for some time, and then allowed me to go and fetch Philip.

I need not have been afraid of the result, though I had prepared him for her extremely blunt way of speaking.

As she shook hands with him, she said,—

'I have come over to see what you are like. I take an interest in this child here, and I was not best pleased at the news. I hope you mean to be good to her. Are you sure you are suited to each other?'

Philip was not in the slightest disconcerted by this speech, only a gleam of humour was in his eye as he replied, 'That remains to be seen. Of course we think we are at present, but that is always the case. I think you will allow I am strong enough to protect her, and old enough to know my own mind. I doubt if I am good enough for her, but I am going to try to do my best.'

Miss Rayner was silent for a minute.

He added, 'I am really glad to meet with any one who takes an interest in Hilda. Her friends seem to be few and far between. She has spoken to me of you, and of how much she enjoyed her visit to you.'

And then they drifted into an easy, amicable conversation one with the other, whilst I for the most part was silent, only putting in a word now and then. Afterwards Mrs. Forsyth came in, and then Miss Rayner did not stay much longer. I had one word alone with her in the hall.

'I see by your anxious eyes what you want to ask,' she said good-naturedly, pinching my cheek as she spoke. 'I am slow to make friends, but he looks honest and good, and is presentable; you might do worse, I suppose; only don't be hurried into a hasty marriage, I implore you. Get to know each other through and through first. Ah! well, you have knocked down one of my castles in the air, but I might have expected it! I am sure I wish you every happiness, child.' A quick sigh followed her words, and then she called out brightly to us as she got into her trap,—

'Come over and dine with me both of you one night; if not now, when next you come down, Mr. Stanton. I suppose you will be continually hovering about this neighbourhood now!'

Amy Le Feuvre

The last day of Philip's visit soon came. I drove down to the station to see him off, but I dreaded the parting.

'You must write to me often, and tell me all about yourself,' he said, trying to speak cheerfully; 'and when Easter comes I have a plan in my head. I shall get a cousin of mine to come down with her husband to Cobham Hall, and then she will help me entertain my visitors. I shall invite all of you down, for I want you to see your future home, childie. Meanwhile, I shall doubtless be able to run down here for a day or two and see you. Mrs. Forsyth has kindly asked me to do so whenever I can.'

'Yes,' I said; 'the future looks very bright to me, almost too bright sometimes, I think. Oh, how good God has been!'

Then after a moment's silence I said, 'I shall miss you so, Philip. It will seem like a dream.'

'You will "dwell deep,"' he said, smiling as he quoted my favourite verse. 'We are not solely dependent on each other's presence for happiness, are we? We shall be able to strengthen each other's hands by prayer.'

He went; and I think others besides me missed him. His presence made itself felt wherever it was. Hugh had behaved very well about our engagement. He said to me, with a grave smile, when first he heard of it,—

'You have gained a friend, and I have lost one. I ought to be vexed, I suppose.'

'Oh no,' I replied; 'your friendship with him remains unchanged. You will find there will be no difference. I cannot be to him what you are, and if he does not spend quite so much time with you now as he has done, it will not always be so.'

But he turned away with a laugh and a shake of his head.

We were very quiet for some time after Philip's departure. Constance went away on a visit to Mr. Stroud's relatives. Kenneth went up to London, and as I was still far from strong, I was left to do very much as I liked, Nelly accompanying her mother when she went out. General Forsyth called me into his study one morning to have a talk over my future.

'Have you any idea in your own head when your marriage is to be? Has Stanton said anything to you about it?'

'I—I don't wish to hurry about it,' I said confusedly; 'he is willing to wait.'

'How long?' demanded my guardian shortly.

'Are you wanting to get rid of me?' I asked, a little vexed by his tone.

'Do not be so foolish!' was the reply. 'I intend, as I have told you before, to treat you as I should one of my daughters; but it seems to me that there is nothing to wait for. Constance is going to be married about Easter. I do not see why that time should not suit you.'

'Oh no,' I cried; and though I had resented them at the time, Miss Rayner's words came before me. 'I would rather wait longer; please let me, if it is not inconvenient to you.'

He said no more, but I wondered much if the Forsyths were relieved at the possibility of my leaving them soon. I said something of the sort to Nelly, who, of course, eagerly

Amy Le Feuvre

disclaimed it. 'Why, Hilda, we shall miss you awfully! I don't know what I shall do, unless I get engaged before you go. Fancy me being left here alone, the old maid of the family! I dare say I shall not marry. I have never seen a single man that I care for yet. Some one asked me the other day if I wasn't jealous of you! So ridiculous! I am sure I would be frightened out of my life by Mr. Stanton. I am very glad he picked upon you. You are just made for each other, you two! I wouldn't have him for my husband for worlds! Sometimes when he is thinking, he looks so severe and cold that he makes me shiver. Grace Dawkin said the other day that he looked like a man with a "dark past." Have you ever asked him about his past, Hilda? Because, really, we know very little about him. Hugh seems to know hardly anything. Mother is satisfied, because she knows he comes of a good family; but he may have murdered some one, or done anything, for all we know!'

I knew it was of no use being angry with Nelly, or I could have scolded her well for her way of talking; she always said out anything and everything that came into her head without a thought of whether her hearers would like it or not. There was a little difficulty at first about my taking my Sunday class again. Mrs. Forsyth had an objection to it, but she finally consented, and only forbade me to visit in any of the cottages if there was sickness. Roddy was well again, and no other cases of diphtheria had been heard of. I promised her I would be careful, and joyfully took up my work again, but found I missed Jim much more than I could have imagined. He had always been so helpful at the class, arranging the seats, keeping an eye on the very little ones, and guiding Kitty Brown to and fro. Poor Kitty missed him dreadfully. 'He never teased me, teacher, like the other boys do; he never said a cross word. I wish sometimes it had been me that was took; but I 'spose I'm not good enough.'

'I think Jesus, perhaps, wants you to do some work for Him that Jim couldn't,' I replied, answering her in much the same way I had been answered myself a short time before.

Here Roddy broke in. 'What's Jim doing, teacher? Mother says singin' hymns. Won't he never get time to write a letter to me? I asked him to.'

'He is doing just what Jesus wants him to, Roddy. You mustn't expect a letter, but you will see him again one day, and that will be better than a letter.'

So the time slipped on, and writing so constantly to Philip and hearing from him in return, was my greatest consolation during his absence. Twice he managed to come down for a couple of days, which were much enjoyed by us both; and then Easter drew near, and with it all the bustle attending the preparations for Constance's wedding. After it was over we were to go down to Cobham Hall, which was Philip's place, and stay there for three or four weeks, and Nelly as well as myself was greatly looking forward to it.

Two days before the wedding we were gathered, a large and merry party, in the drawing-room after dinner. Philip had come down that afternoon, but in spite of his pleasure at being with us again, I fancied he was ill at ease, and wondered at the cause.

'Now, Goody Two-Shoes,' Kenneth cried, when music was going on, 'give us something extra nice from your fiddle. Get into a dream over it, and make us all as dreamy as yourself.'

I took my violin up, and standing in my favourite position against one of the French windows I began to play. Everything that evening is stamped vividly upon my memory. I can see now the yellow jasmine outside the windows

Amy Le Feuvre

fluttering to and fro in the breeze, the lilacs and laburnums on the lawn sending some of their sweet fragrance through one of the half-opened doors, and the last rays of the setting sun gilding the tops of the distant hills. As I turned my eyes inwards, I saw a bright fire, General Forsyth on one side reading the evening paper, Mrs. Forsyth on the other, busy with her fancy work and little table before her. At the piano, lounging about in different attitudes, were Nelly and several girl cousins, Kenneth and two other gentlemen in the background, whilst at the farther window stood Constance with Mr. Stroud. Philip was bending over a book with Hugh at a small table near, but when I began to play he threw himself into an easy chair, and resting his head upon his hand, prepared himself to listen. I noted an abstracted, moody look in his eyes, and it was in vain that he tried to hide it. I began to play one of Beethoven's sonatas, but drifted on from that to my own fancies, and glancing out into the dusky twilight, seemed to feel, rather than see, great banks of heavy, gloomy clouds roll up and envelop us in their darkness. A strange depression seemed to take possession of me, a heavy weight to settle down upon my spirits. I played on dreamily, until suddenly I was stopped by a cry from Constance, 'Do for pity's sake stop that wail, Hilda; one would think you were playing our funeral dirge!'

Her sharp tone so startled me that my violin fell to the ground with a crash. I gave a shiver, and Kenneth said, 'Has an evil spirit taken possession of you, Goody? You have put us all into the blues by the uncanny cries and moans that have proceeded from your fiddle! What is the matter with you?'

I could not answer him, Philip was picking up and replacing my violin in its case, after which he laid his hand on my arm. 'Come into the library with me.'

I followed him; he stirred up the fire, which was nearly out, and then drew me to him.

'What is the matter, childie?'

Nothing could have been more tender than his tone. The tears came to my eyes, and I rested my head against his shoulder with a sigh.

'I don't know,' I said. 'What is the matter with you, Philip?'

'You have sharp eyes to see that anything is the matter,' he replied, smiling; then, in a graver tone, he added, 'I have something worrying me—a matter of business that I cannot speak of at present to you. You must trust me, Hilda. Can you do this, do you think, even if appearances are against me?'

He raised my face to his as he spoke, and our eyes met. Trust him! I felt as I met his clear, open gaze that I would trust him through any amount of doubt or mystery, and I told him as much as we stood by the firelight together.

'I wish,' he said presently, 'that it was our wedding that was going to take place to-morrow; and yet I don't know—perhaps it will be best for you that it is not.'

A heavy sigh followed, and then we were both startled by the appearance of a servant.

'A telegram, sir.'

Philip took it and turned to me.

'I must leave you. Darling child, don't look so distressed. I am vexed that I should have to go before the wedding, but it

Amy Le Feuvre

is imperative that I should. I must write and tell you my movements when I know them. I shall just catch the 10.30 train to town if I go at once. Hilda, say good-bye to me here before I go to the drawing-room. Trust me, little one, and pray for me.'

I clung to him, for I still felt the shadow of a dark cloud hovering over us. 'Why need you go? Where are you going? When are you coming back again? We were to have travelled to your home together. Don't go till you have told me more, Philip. You *must* not leave me like this!'

He looked surprised at my vehemence. 'Dear child, you are overwrought. I shall be back in a few days at the most, I hope. Good-bye, my darling; God bless you and keep you!' And taking me in his arms, he kissed me over and over again. I said no more, my tongue seemed tied, and he left me standing by the fire, feeling as if a great unknown trouble was settling down upon me.

I stayed there, heard his voice in the hall, and then a confused babel of questions and exclamations from the others. When, a few minutes later, I heard him leave the house, I flew upstairs to my room; I knew from my window I should see a bend of the road along which he must pass, and as I saw the trap driving rapidly along I leant out and waved my handkerchief. He saw my signal. I suppose the light in my room and the unclosed shutters to the windows helped him to do so, and taking up the lantern in front of the trap he waved it to me. Then came a knock at my door, and Mrs. Forsyth appeared. 'Do you know the reason of this sudden disappearance, Hilda? I do wish sometimes Mr. Stanton were a little more communicative.'

'It was a telegram,' I said, trying to speak quietly; 'only a matter of business, he said, but it obliged him to go to

London immediately.'

'It is very annoying. I was quite counting on his presence to-morrow. We seem to have such a scarcity of men. Are you not coming down to the drawing-room again?'

'I would rather not, please,' I said; for I felt I could not go through all the questions and remarks that would assail me.

Mrs. Forsyth did not stay, and I, trying to fight with the nameless fears in my heart, took refuge and comfort in prayer.

CHAPTER XVI

DARK DAYS

'Rest thou in God, amid all changes;
Be pleased with all He may ordain;
Wait patient till what He arranges,
For thy best welfare shall be plain;
God who has chosen us as His,
Knows best what our true welfare is.'

—Neumark

The wedding passed off successfully. I think I was the only one who felt out of harmony with the brightness and gaiety all around. Though the Forsyths felt the loss of their eldest daughter, there was much to soften their regret at parting with her. She was not going very far away from them; she and her husband seemed exactly suited to each other in many ways, and she was going to a comfortable, luxurious home.

I think too that Nelly occupied a warmer place in their hearts than Constance. The latter seemed to live so entirely for herself, and her nature was so cold and unsympathetic that her presence did not always make home the happier for it. Nelly was the sunshine of the house, and it was she who up to the last kept up an atmosphere of sparkling brightness which none could withstand.

We felt rather 'flat,' as Kenneth expressed it, when all was over and the guests had departed. My thoughts were with Philip, and when, two days after his departure, the post brought me a letter in his handwriting, I opened it with trembling fingers. It was very short.

'MY DARLING,—

'I am off to America on this business that I spoke to you about. Will send you my address later on, but my movements are quite uncertain. So sorry that your visit to Cobham Hall must be postponed. God bless you!

'Yours 'PHILIP.'

I had expected something of this sort, and was hardly surprised, though I did wish he had written more fully. When I told the others, I had to bear a great deal of comment and commiseration.

'I cannot bear mysteries,' said General Forsyth; 'why can't the fellow tell his business instead of being so vague about it?'

'He is so exceedingly reticent about his affairs,' said Mrs. Forsyth, 'that one seems to know very little more about him now than one did at first. Are you in his confidence, Hugh?'

'If I were, I would be hardly likely to betray what he sees best to withhold.'

Hugh's tone was haughty. I looked across the breakfast table at him with a smile, feeling I had one on my side to do battle for the absent one.

Amy Le Feuvre

'It's awfully disappointing,' grumbled Nelly. 'I was looking forward to our visit at his place, and have refused several invitations that I might have had instead of it. When people go off to America they generally stay there for years, and are never heard of any more.'

'That is cheerful for me,' I said, forcing a laugh; 'but America is not very far off, Nelly, the passage takes next to no time, it is only a question of a few weeks.'

'It is well to keep up your spirits, Goody, but it looks bad— very bad!' and Kenneth shook his head with mock solemnity as he spoke. 'We all noticed his gloom and uneasiness the last evening he was here. I am afraid he has a "dark past," and his conscience is troubling him. Be prepared for the worst. It may be a case of another woman, Goody. In the style of the penny dreadfuls, a wife that he thought dead may have turned up again, and then where would you be? He may have been married two or three times before, for all we know!'

'That will do,' General Forsyth said sternly; 'such jokes are extremely out of place, and we will have no more of them.'

And Kenneth subsided, to my great relief. I felt I could bear very little more, and was glad to get away alone and bear my disappointment as best I could.

But the next few weeks were very trying ones. Not for an instant did I doubt Philip, but others did, and the remarks and conjectures on his sudden departure were hard for me to sit and listen to.

I did not hear from him again, except a post-card to announce his arrival in New York. I wrote to him there, but received no answer, and the time of waiting and suspense seemed interminable.

If I had not learnt the secret of 'dwelling deep' in dark times, I sometimes think I should not have been able to live through that time. The Forsyths were kind, and felt for me, I knew; but my guardian was angry by the suddenness of it all, and persisted in looking upon me as being ill-treated in the matter. Nelly took the very blackest view, and declared I would never hear of or see him again, whilst Kenneth spent his time in concocting the most elaborate stories and bringing them out for my benefit, of different people who mysteriously disappeared, and the causes of their doing so. Hugh was the only one who with me felt it must be right, and he often cheered me by assurances of his speedy return.

'It is most likely money matters,' he said one day to me; 'I know a good deal of his income is in some funds in New York. He has some cousin in business there, who manages things for him.'

And this was the most likely solution I could obtain. But why did he not write? As time went on I grew more and more anxious. I said very little to any one, and tried to be cheerful, and go on with my daily life as before, but it was a hard matter.

I could not bring myself to touch my violin. That last evening rose up before me, and the dim foreboding of evil that had so overshadowed me. I felt a strange shrinking from the very thing that used to be such a comfort and delight to me.

One afternoon I was startled by a message being brought to me by Miss Rayner's old coachman, saying she was ill and wanted to see me. Mrs. Forsyth had gone up to London for a fortnight, so I went at once to my guardian.

Amy Le Feuvre

'Helen ill!' he exclaimed. 'I should not think she has had a day's illness in her life. What is the matter with her?'

'John says she fell into the river trying to ford it riding, and did not change her wet things. He says she got a violent chill last week, and has had a great deal of fever. This is her note to me.'

I gave him a little slip of paper, on which was scrawled, in letters very unlike Miss Rayner's usually firm hand:—

'DEAR HILDA,—

'I am ill. Will you come and help Susan to nurse me?

'Yours affectionately,

'HELEN RAYNER.'

General Forsyth gave his consent to my going, and I returned that afternoon with John, who was full of garrulous accounts of Miss Rayner's illness. He wound up with saying,—

'And h'it's just my doing that hi'm taking you back. I said to Susan this morning,—I won't be a party to hiding h'it h'any longer. I'll go straight over to the general's and get some one to come h'and see to her while she's yet h'alive, and you may tell the mistress that hi'm doing it. So Susan she sees hi'm not to be trifled with, h'and she tells Miss Helen, h'and she sends this note for you. You will find her very h'ill, miss. She's been at death's door, h'and she's not turned the corner yet!'

The house was very still when we entered it. Even the dogs seemed to know something was the matter, for there was no bounding forward and barking when I appeared; they only crept up to me, and looked with mute, wistful appeal into my face, as if to ask for their absent mistress. As I went quietly up the stairs I met the doctor coming down. He looked grave, and, in answer to my inquiries, said,—

'I hope she will pull through; the worst has passed, but she is very weak. If you are going to be with her, do not let her talk too much. She must not be excited; and see that she has nourishment at the times I have ordered. I shall be in early to-morrow morning.'

A minute after and I stood by her bedside, but I was shocked to see how her illness had pulled her down. She lay motionless, but not asleep, and when I laid my hand softly upon hers she looked up.

'Do you know me?' she asked, with a faint smile. 'I feel a wreck, and as helpless as a baby!'

'I wish we had known about it before,' I said, 'I would have come over at once.'

'I was too ill to care,' she responded. 'I hate people fussing round. I thought I should like to see you, and so sent John over.'

She closed her eyes, and I, quietly removing my hat and jacket, came and took up my position at the bedside.

Susan and I had some anxious days after this, and, beyond saying a verse or two from the Bible to her, I could do nothing but pray for her. She seemed too weak to be able to hear or understand. But at length she really began to mend, and then her recovery was rapid.

One afternoon, the first time I felt I could with safety let her talk a little to me, she turned to me and said abruptly,—

'Hilda, I can't face death. I am not prepared for it.'

I did not answer for a minute, then I said,—

'God has been very good in saving you from that, hasn't He?'

'But I have been on the brink of it, child, and I can't forget it. It has made me see things so differently—my wasted life, and my self-will and self-pleasing, my rejection of so much Bible truth that was distasteful to me. I have thought and thought over these things till I wonder I did not go crazy. It was that that made me send for you. I felt you were the only one that could help me.'

'I am afraid I have not been able to do much,' I responded. 'You have been too ill to talk to, but I have been praying for you.'

'You said one verse to me soon after you came that has been ringing in my head ever since. Wasn't it something like this, "There is one Mediator between God and men, the man Christ Jesus, in whom we have redemption through His blood, even the forgiveness of sins"?'

'Yes,' I replied; 'but those are bits of verses you have put together. I repeated both of them to you.'

I took my Bible and read them to her again, then she said,—

'Now then, take those verses as your text, and give me a little discourse on them, just as you do to your little Sunday scholars.'

I hesitated. Never had I been asked to do anything that seemed as difficult as this. Yet I dared not refuse such an opportunity, and, with an earnest prayer for the Holy Spirit's guidance, I began, falteringly enough at first, to talk about it. I do not remember now what I said; I was only conscious at the time of Miss Rayner's earnest gaze, and of a longing desire that she might obtain both pardon and peace.

She listened in silence, then said,—

'Now I want to hear you pray. Don't look so frightened. You pray with the old villagers you go to see, and I have a soul as much as they have. Kneel down and pray for me.'

I knelt, and when I rose she had tears in her eyes.

'You are a dear little thing!' she said in a softened tone; 'one would think my welfare was as precious to you as your own, to hear you! Now, that is enough for to-day. Suppose you leave me, and go out into the garden for a breath of fresh air. You can send Susan to me.'

I stooped and kissed her before I left, saying softly,—

'Dear Miss Rayner, I know you will find Him if you seek Him. He is very near you now.'

We had several talks together after that. I could not help thanking God again and again for having given me this bit of work in the midst of my own trouble. And it was touching to see how, with all her power of intellect and will, Miss Rayner's illness had humbled her like a little child. She seemed to realize deeply her sin in rejecting the truth for so long.

It was when she was beginning to sit up a little that one day she turned to me and said, 'I have not asked after Mr. Stanton once yet. When are you going to Cobham Hall?'

She evidently knew nothing of what had taken place, and was greatly surprised when I told her all.

'Do you mean to say you have never heard from him since he left?' she exclaimed.

'Yes, once—from New York. That is nearly two months ago.'

'I wish you hadn't been so quick about it, child. I felt from the commencement that it was a risky thing, your knowing so very little about him!'

'I know him well enough to be able to trust him,' I said quietly.

She looked at me and smiled. 'Then you are not anxious, at all events?'

'Yes, I am anxious,' I replied, 'for I do not understand his silence. He must be ill, or something must have happened to him; but other people do not think so, and their insinuations and remarks about it are almost more than I can bear.'

Miss Rayner was silent. I added impulsively, 'I had more than once thought of writing to you, and asking you to have me for a little. I felt it would be such a relief to get away from all the talk. This was before I knew you were ill, of course.'

'And why did you not?'

'I thought it would be rather selfish of me. Now Constance is married, Nelly seems to cling more to me, and there is my work in the village. It is rather cowardly to run away from one's duties if the way is not smooth, don't you think so?'

Miss Rayner did not answer, only said with a sigh a moment after, 'I hope he will not disappoint you.'

Amy Le Feuvre

CHAPTER XVII

DAWN

'The night is mother of the day,
The winter of the spring.'

Mrs. Forsyth came to see her sister directly she returned from town, and was vexed that she had not been sent for before. She was quite willing that I should remain where I was, and so after she had returned home again I had some quiet, restful weeks during Miss Rayner's convalescence. I call them restful, but though I had the sense of peace and rest deep down in my heart, I am afraid on the surface I was restless and ill at ease. Every post awakened fresh expectation and hope, only to be followed by the depression of disappointment. I prayed much to be given a quiet mind, and I do think, to some extent, my prayer was answered. And I had the intense joy of seeing Miss Rayner's whole life change, her interests and thoughts now centred on things above. She did not say much, but her Bible was now her constant companion, and I felt by her conversation how real and deep the change was in her.

It was one evening in the beginning of July that we were sitting out in a low verandah that ran along one side of the house. The sun was setting in front of us, and a glorious sunset it was; the sky was illuminated with rosy light from the deepest crimson to the most delicate pink, and the fleecy clouds that passed by seemed bathed in its golden splendour.

'It always makes me think of heaven's gates,' I was saying to Miss Rayner; but before she had time to reply we were startled by the sudden appearance of Hugh.

In a moment I was on my feet, and I felt every vestige of colour leave my face.

'You have some news!' I cried.

For answer he quietly put a letter in my hand, and when I saw the well-known writing the reaction was too much, I sat down and burst into a flood of tears.

Miss Rayner wisely left me alone. She drew Hugh away, and took him inside the drawing-room, saying, 'It has been a strain to the child—this time of suspense, though she has taken it so quietly. She will be better left to herself.'

And then when they had left me I opened my letter. It had evidently met with some delay on the road, for it was written a long time past. Only one sheet as follows:—

'MY DEAREST,—

'How you must have wondered at my silence, and how little I thought what a test your love and trust would be put to during this long time! When I reached New York I found it imperative to push on somewhere in these remote regions, from where I date this letter. I had only time to send you a card, but I little thought how long it would be before you would hear from me again. A bad accident resulted in my being stretched on a sick-bed for two whole months, and I am only now able to write. But I am on the way to speedy recovery now, and as soon as I can be moved I shall make the best of my way home to you. The business I was called out here about is at an end. Circumstances have made me wonder, as I lie on my bed, whether it is still right to allow you to link your life with mine. But I cannot write it. I must see you face to face, if God permits, and then we must talk it over. I am hoping to be in England soon after you receive this. Till then, darling, good-bye.

'Ever yours, 'P. STANTON.'

I sat with the letter in my hand, one thought after another following in rapid succession. But what really filled me with anxiety and dismay was the date on which the letter was posted. According to his statement he ought to have arrived in England long before this, and why had he not done so?

I rose from my seat and called Miss Rayner, who came to my side at once.

'Well? Good news, I hope!' she said cheerily.

'Why isn't he here?' I said, and I handed her the letter. She read it, and told Hugh its contents, as I did not seem to have the voice to speak.

'He may have been delayed,' Hugh said at once, 'I will go up to his agents again in town, and find out if they know anything of his movements.'

'Again!' I exclaimed. 'Have you been before then?'

'Yes,' he said hesitatingly; 'there was nothing to tell you, or I would have done so. They had lost sight of him themselves.'

'When did you go?' I demanded, 'and what did they say? Oh! Hugh! you might have told me. I didn't know he had any agents in town, or I would have gone myself. Let me come with you now—tonight.'

Miss Rayner laid her hand on my arm. 'Don't be so excited, child. Use a little of your common sense. Do you think there is any chance of getting up to town at this time of night, or if there were, would you be likely to get the information you need? Hugh can sleep here, and go up the first thing tomorrow morning.'

To this Hugh agreed at once. He seemed almost as anxious as I for the welfare of his friend.

The letter had brought little comfort to me, but I could see it had greatly relieved Miss Rayner's mind. My one fear now was that it was illness, perhaps death, that was the cause of his absence.

'He says so little,' I remarked presently; 'he does not tell me the nature of the accident, or how badly he has been hurt. And why should the letter have been delayed?'

'That is easily accounted for,' said Hugh, taking up the envelope and examining the post-mark. 'He was evidently at some rough mountain place when he wrote, and posts are few and far between. If you trust your letters to a messenger or a passer-by, you may think yourself fortunate if he remembers to post them at all, and they may often lie in his coat pocket for weeks before he thinks of them.'

That was an anxious evening to me. As I was wishing Hugh 'good-night' I said, 'I have never thanked you yet for coming over to me at once with the letter. It was very good of you.'

'The governor suggested posting it, but I thought you would like to get it as soon as possible. Nell was dying to open it; she told me to tell you she wanted you home again. When are you going to part with her, aunt?' And he turned towards Miss Rayner as he spoke.

'When she wants to go,' was the blunt reply.

I went to bed soon after, but I could not sleep. I read and re-read the letter, and wished much that further details had been given. Yet when I thought of him penning those lines on a sick-bed, perhaps with the greatest difficulty and pain, I could wish he had not troubled to write so much. Earnestly did I pray that his health and strength might be given back to him. I felt it such a comfort to pour out all my doubts and fears to God, knowing that He was not only willing to listen, but able to control all Himself, and watch over and protect, yes, and heal the absent one. I fell asleep, repeating to myself, 'The steps of a good man are ordered by the Lord,' and it brought comfort to my soul.

Hugh was off the first thing the next morning, but Miss Rayner would not allow me to go up to town with him, and it seemed the longest day that I had ever spent. Miss Rayner asked me if I would like to return to the Forsyths at once, but I shook my head.

'You are not quite strong yet,' I said to her, 'and I do like being here. I feel as if they will be so full of questions, and will pick my letter to pieces, if I go back. General Forsyth always imagines the worst about people. None of them believed it must be illness that caused his silence, though I felt myself it must be. They all ascribed the worst motives they could think of for it. And—and sometimes I feel I can't forgive them for doubting and mistrusting him so.'

'You don't mean that?' Miss Rayner said, looking at me steadily.

'No,' I said, colouring a little, 'I have no ill-feeling really, I ought not to have harboured it for an instant, but it would come. I try and look at it from their side, and of course I know that what you all say is true. A few months ago he was a stranger; oh! Miss Rayner, tell me, do you fear the worst? If he is dead, I think my heart will break!'

'Hearts are not so easily broken,' Miss Rayner replied, with a little sigh; 'my dear, you must have patience and wait. I think most likely he has only been delayed. You would have heard before now if the worst had happened.'

Hugh returned about eight o'clock that evening, but he had little news to give us. Philip's agents had known only quite recently of his illness, and were expecting to hear of his arrival in England every day.

So there was nothing for me to do but wait patiently. I left Miss Rayner soon after, for the Forsyths wanted me back.

'I shall miss you, child,' she said, as we were parting, 'and you must pray for me. I find that the habits of a lifetime are not easily uprooted; if I get into a tangle, I shall send for my little minister to put me straight again.'

'No; you don't want any one to come between you and God,' I said with a smile; but I left her with a heavy heart. We had grown, in spite of the disparity between our ages, to be such very close friends since her illness.

And then I took up my old life again, hoping every day to hear fresh tidings, and trying to bear the disappointment as brightly and bravely as I could.

Amy Le Feuvre

One afternoon I wandered out by myself to the moor. It was a hot day in August, but there was always a breeze up there, and I loved to get away from every one; the loveliness and stillness soothed and comforted me. I had my Bible with me, and the hours slipped by so quickly that when I began to retrace my way homewards I found it was much later than I had imagined. At the entrance to the village I met Kenneth. 'Well, you are a nice one!' was his remark when he saw me; 'do you know we have been scouring the country for you all the afternoon? A telegram came for you about a quarter of an hour after you had left the house—Goodness gracious! are you going to faint? There's nothing wrong—allow me to finish my sentence—and now there's something better than a telegram arrived in the shape of a two-legged specimen—'

'He has come then!' I exclaimed. 'Oh, Kenneth, tell me!'

'Who has come? Who are you expecting? You interrupt me so that I have lost the thread of my discourse, and forget what I was going to say.'

Then seeing that I was not in a state to stand much more joking, he altered his tone. 'Yes, he has arrived, looking rather seedy, but he is alive. He has been closeted with the governor for the last two hours, giving an account of himself. I hope it is all fair and square, but he won't let us into his secrets, though I told him his conduct had been rather "fishy" in our eyes. What are you going to do? Run away from me? You are such a dignified little soul generally, that I expected we should have a saunter up to the house together; but I forgot that "love lends wings," isn't that the saying? I will race you if you like. Now, one, two, three, and away!'

And in another minute we were tearing through the village and up the avenue to the house in a style that would have greatly shocked Mrs. Forsyth, had she seen us. Kenneth gave a loud 'whoop' when we entered the hall, which brought every one out at once, but I was only conscious of one form, one greeting, and the next minute I found myself drawn into the empty library. Then my composure gave way: clinging hold of him, I could do nothing but sob, and for some minutes there was perfect silence between us. I could only feel the touch of his fingers on my hair, and the strong beating of his heart, against which my head was resting.

And then I controlled myself, and looked up into his face. 'Oh, Philip, how ill you must have been! How worn and ill you look! Are you well again?'

'Very nearly well, thank God!' was the reply. 'And now come and sit down, childie, here by me, and let me tell you everything. You have never doubted me, have you? I need not ask you, for your eyes tell me. Only you are looking white and thin, darling. The suspense must have tried you!'

'It is all right now,' I said. 'I am longing to hear it all.'

But Philip's explanation had to be postponed—the gong rang for dinner, and I knew we must not keep the others waiting.

As I went up to my room to change my dress, Nelly seized hold of me. 'Oh, Hilda, I'm so glad for you! And it will come all right, though father is shaking his head downstairs, and saying to mother he doubts whether he ought to countenance your engagement proceeding. What is it? has he lost money?'

'I don't know,' I answered,' and I don't care. I only know he is safe home again, that is quite enough for me at present!'

CHAPTER XVIII

WEDDED

'My wife, my life. O we will walk this world
Yoked, in all exercise of noble end,...
Indeed I love thee, come
Yield thyself up: my hopes and thine are one.'

—Tennyson

It was after dinner, wandering arm-in-arm through the dusky garden, that Philip told me the whole story. It appeared that a young cousin of his whom he had promised a dying mother to befriend, had fallen into bad company out in New York, and had accomplished several successful forgeries for very large amounts in Philip's name. He was clerk in a house of business out there with which Philip was connected; in fact, he had obtained the situation for him. The forgeries were discovered whilst Philip was with us, and though he forbade any proceedings to be taken until he had investigated the matter himself, Ronald Stanton, the culprit, took fright and absconded, taking with him a great deal of money from the firm in which he was. And Philip on the impulse of the moment determined to follow his track and save him if possible from worse ruin. It was the wish to shield this cousin that kept him silent, and made him leave us with so little explanation. When he arrived at New York, he told the managers of the firm that he would be responsible for the missing sums, and started with a confidential servant in quest of the runaway. He went through a variety of adventures before he came on his track, and then at length when he met him in the depths of some backwoods, the young fellow turned upon him in desperation, and before Philip could explain that it was on an errand of mercy and not of justice that he had followed him, in the heat of the moment Ronald drew his revolver and shot him.

'It was very nearly proving fatal for me,' said Philip as he told the story, 'but God in His mercy prevented the sin of murder being laid to the poor lad's charge. He was in such a state of mind when he found what he had done, that if it had not been for my servant's restraining hand, he would have made an attempt on his own life. I could just manage to say, "I have come to save you," and then I remembered no more; but when I recovered consciousness I found that he had become my watchful, untiring nurse. I think it was due to his indefatigable care that I recovered. Both he and my man Dawson never left me night or day. Poor fellow! it was as I feared. He had been a mere tool in the hands of others, who had decamped, leaving him to bear the consequences of his sin.'

'But, Philip, how long were you ill? And were you hurt much? I have no pity for your cousin—no, none; how could he, oh, how could he treat you so?'

'Perhaps I had better tell you no more. Let us talk of other things.'

'No, no, I want to hear everything; please go on.'

'I tried to write to you when I got better, for I thought you

Amy Le Feuvre

would be less alarmed than if a stranger wrote to you; but in illness one does not take much count of time, and I had no idea that I had left you so long without a line. At last I was able to manage, and then I did hope I should get home. Ronald, poor boy, waited to come back and give himself up to the hands of justice, and in telling your guardian about it he thinks I was wrong in not letting the law take its course. But I would be the only sufferer, it was my money he had made away with, and I could bear the loss. He was so thoroughly and truly repentant that I did not regret it. I made arrangements for him to go and start life afresh out there on a farm. It is his determination to pay back gradually as he can all he owes; but this would be the work of a lifetime. It was through gambling that he was tempted first of all.'

'But why did you not come home at once?'

'I had a relapse, and found when I reached the nearest town I must go into hospital to have the bullet extracted, which had never been done. I did send you a letter from there, which you ought to have had, but an accident happened to some mail bags about that time; they got burnt, and I can only conclude yours must have been amongst them.'

'And were you very ill in hospital?'

'I had rather a bad time of it. If I had been able to have a proper doctor at the time, it would have saved me a good deal. As it is, my right lung has been injured, and I shall have to be careful for a long time.'

'I feel as if I can never forgive that cousin of yours, never! Oh! Philip, why were you so good to him?' And unnerved by the account he had given me, I burst into tears.

'It has been too much for you to-night, childie,' and Philip drew me closer to him. 'You will feel differently towards him to-morrow. I have told you all, for you have a right to know, and I found I was obliged to tell your guardian; but I did it in the strictest confidence, and I know he will respect my wishes about it. Others need not know particulars, and you must try to forget it. Now to come to the subject that will concern us much more closely. This has made a difference in my prospects. I have not gone thoroughly into my affairs yet, but I see nothing for it but to let Cobham for a few years. I will not go into debt, neither will I mortgage it, and I cannot now afford to keep the place up as it should be. I think eventually I shall be able to go back to it, but not at present. Will you be content with a small house somewhere near town, while I follow my literary pursuits, as much now for gain as formerly for pleasure?'

'Why do you ask me such a question? you know how satisfied I shall be.'

'The general is not. He is very distressed about it, and then there is another objection now—my health.' He stopped, and his face looked grave and worn in the', dusky twilight. I stood still and faced him, a dreadful fear taking possession of me.

'Philip, tell me truly, is your life in danger? are the doctors afraid of anything serious?'

He took my hands in both his, as he answered, 'There is nothing to be anxious about, my darling, at present. I shall need care and nursing, perhaps. They give me hope that time will outgrow the mischief, but perhaps it may shorten my life. I tell you this because I want you to see what is before us. I have no right to expect you to link your life with mine under these circumstances, and your guardian is very doubtful as to the wisdom and expediency of it.'

Amy Le Feuvre

'Does he think,' I said, the blood rushing to my cheeks with indignation, 'that this will make any difference in my feeling towards you? It will certainly in one way; it will make me ten times more conscious of the honour it will be to become your wife. It will make me realize more and more your unselfish devotion and goodness towards the one who has marred and spoilt your life, and make me know what a noble—'

'Hush! hush!' he said, half laughing, as he dropped my hands, and put his arm round me, 'you may think me a hero to-night, but in the calm light of to-morrow morning you may think differently. And yet I am so confident of your love and trust that I have never doubted how you would act. I would not let you sacrifice yourself, if I were sure in my own heart that my health was seriously injured; but I do not think it is. I believe the doctors are right when they say that time will heal the mischief. I do not think we shall be called to give each other up, if you are content to take me as I am.'

Much more we said to each other on that calm, still evening; and before we came indoors we gave thanks together to our Heavenly Father for His goodness in bringing us together again.

I was obliged to have an interview with my guardian the next morning. He was very kind, but said he was doubtful whether, under the present circumstances, I ought not to look at things with a different eye. When he found, as I think he must have expected to find, my opinions on the subject were totally unchanged, he ended up by saying, 'Of course I have tried to act towards you as I should towards my own daughters. It is a disappointment to me that you will not be as comfortably off with Stanton as I had supposed you would be at first, and there is his state of health that is a drawback; but still I cannot press you to break off the engagement, having given my sanction to it. I only wish he had not acted in the extraordinary quixotic way he has. Then all this trouble might have been spared you both. For a man of his age and stamp, I consider he has been most foolish, if not to say culpable, in the manner he has treated that young scoundrel of a cousin!'

Two evenings after this we were in the drawing-room after dinner, when Philip asked me if I would play to them.

There was silence amongst the others whilst I opened my violin case, and then Kenneth remarked, as I began to tighten the strings, 'Can it ever be used again? Don't you know, Stanton, that it was not only a broken heart, but a broken fiddle you left behind you, when you departed so suddenly last time you were here? It's astonishing how soon hearts get mended, and fiddles too, it appears. Goody has shuddered at the sight of that instrument ever since. I thought the epitaph on her tombstone would be, "She never played again!"'

I found a difficulty in playing that night in the midst of this nonsense. I seemed to have lived a lifetime since last I had touched my violin; but when I had once started, I as usual forgot everything but just the comfort and soothing it brought me. And when I had finished, Nelly said, impulsively, 'There! now you look like your old self, Hilda. You haven't been the same since that night Kenneth was speaking of. Don't you love your violin? I am sure you do, from the way you handle it!'

'Of course I love it,' I responded warmly.

Kenneth laughed. 'You have a rival, Stanton. I tell you, when she stands up there, her eyes getting bigger and bigger, and her precious fiddle hugged tighter and tighter, you are absolutely nowhere—out of her affections and thoughts altogether! I think, if I were in your place, I should quietly make away with it when you have an opportunity. It will bring discord into your life, I warn you; it is capable of it!'

We all laughed; but Philip said to me afterwards, 'Everything that I see and hear makes me realize afresh what an anxiety and strain I have brought into your life. Can you forgive me?'

'Is there anything to forgive?' I asked. 'I have been anxious, Philip—it was no wonder, but I think the trouble and anxiety has only made me realize the force and strength of that verse in the Psalms, as I never should have done otherwise: "God is our refuge and strength, a very present help in trouble."'

'And it is worth going through the darkness to experience His tenderness and care,' was the rejoinder.

Philip had a great deal of business to do for the next month or two, and then it was settled that our marriage should take place the latter end of November. A dreary month for a wedding generally, but it was not so in our case, and it was a sunshiny, frosty morning when we stood together in the little village church as man and wife.

I could not have believed, if any one had told me a twelvemonth before, how much I should have felt the parting with the Forsyths—Nelly especially lay very near to my heart; we had had many a talk together of things above, and I sometimes dared to hope that she had grasped hold of the truth, though she was fearful of letting others know about it. The night before our wedding she came to me and asked me to pray with her, which I did; and then with tears in her eyes she said, 'I shall miss you so dreadfully, Hilda; you have helped me to see things so differently, and I don't think I shall ever be satisfied now with just a whirl of gaiety.'

'You have promised to take my Sunday class, so that will give you an interest,' I said, trying to speak brightly; 'and oh! Nelly, if you get to know the Lord as your personal Friend, you won't miss me. He will be quite sufficient.'

'I am trying to,' she said softly; 'I would like to know Him as you do.' Then in a brisker tone she said, 'And you will ask me to stay with you soon, won't you? When you are in town, you know! I should like to come, and I won't ask to go to any theatres, or even to a picture gallery, or a ride in the Row, if you think it worldly! But do let me come just to be with you.'

Miss Graham bid me good-bye with much grief; but I felt happy about her; she was steadfastly setting her face heavenwards, and praying and influencing her pupil into the same path too. I think Mrs. Forsyth was genuinely sorry for me to leave, and when I said something to her about being so sorry that my views had clashed with hers, and hoping she would understand how it was, she gave me a warm kiss, saying, 'Never mind the past, my dear. Perhaps if I had been brought up differently, I should have seen more with you. We shall miss you very much, for you have been a great help and comfort to us whilst you have been here.'

Miss Rayner appeared at the wedding, to every one's great astonishment. Her parting words caused me much thought and consideration: 'Don't be surprised if you hear soon that I have given up my chicks, and departed to the wilds of Africa as a missionary. I must do something with my bit of wasted life left me.'

My little Sunday scholars were in full force at the church gate as we went through, and irrepressible Roddy darted up to me and clutched hold of my dress,—'You isn't going away to heaven, is you, like Jim?'

Amy Le Feuvre

'Not yet, I think,' I answered, trying to detach his chubby fingers from my skirt.

'I thought you was, in that booful angel dress!' And he fell back with a trace of disappointment on his rosy face.

Kitty was by his side openly weeping. As I came down the path after it was all over, I could not help giving her a special 'good-bye.' Her sad little face flushed with pleasure as I did so, and she murmured, 'I never shall forget you, teacher, you've taught me to love Jesus'; and my own eyes filled with tears at her words.

As we drove away to the station on our way to the Continent for a month or six weeks, and I felt I was on the threshold of a new life, I said to Philip, 'I feel as if I could put to this chapter of my life, "Not one thing hath failed of all the good things which the Lord God spake concerning you!"'

CHAPTER XIX

OLD FRIENDS

'One in heart, in interest and design,
Gird up each other to the race divine.'

—Cowper

'Hilda, I have an old friend coming to dine with us to-night. I came across him in town to-day; you are sure to like him, he is a general favourite wherever he goes.'

'What is his name?'

'Ratcliffe—Charles Ratcliffe. I have known him a long time, before he cared for serious things. It was a meeting in town to which I took him that was, in God's hands, the means of his conversion. That was many years ago, when I was just beginning to understand these things; I was quite a young fellow myself, and he is my senior by many years. I shall like you to know him, and I want him to know my wife.'

We were at breakfast, and it was a cold morning in February. Philip had taken a flat in South Kensington, and though in many ways we should have preferred a house of our own, we were perfectly happy with this arrangement. The only anxiety I had was Philip's health; his lung that had been so affected still gave him trouble, and he was often confined to the house for weeks at a time. All day long I kept repeating the name of Charles Ratcliffe over to myself, and wondering where I had heard it before, but it was not until our guest was actually in our drawing-room, and shaking hands with me, that it flashed across me. Miss Rayner had been engaged to a Mr. Ratcliffe. Could this be the same, I wondered? And I determined presently to find out. He was a tall, handsome man with an iron-grey moustache and clear blue eyes. I could not keep my gaze off him. How often I had longed that somehow or other I might be permitted to bring those two together again! It would be strange if I were to discover that he was the identical man.

Our conversation got round to the Forsyths and their part of the country, and then I said boldly, 'One of the prettiest parts is where Mrs. Forsyth's sister lives, a Miss Rayner. She lives in an old farmhouse close to the moor. I spent some of my happiest days with her.'

He did not start or show any emotion at the name, as I hoped he would; but he said slowly, after a minute's pause, 'I used to know a Miss Rayner long ago—Helen Rayner her name was. I suppose it is the same, as I heard she had settled down there somewhere.'

'She is a very great friend of mine,' I said warmly; 'but I do not think she will be there much longer now, she talks of giving the place up. In fact, she is coming up to town to stay with us next week for a few days, whilst she is meditating an interview with some missionary society; she wants to go abroad as a missionary. Perhaps, as you are old friends, Mr. Ratcliffe, you would like to meet her. Won't you come and dine with us again whilst she is here? Would next Friday suit you?'

I saw Philip glance across at me with slight surprise; but I was too intent on my own plan to mind, and he at once added his invitation to mine.

Mr. Ratcliffe hesitated a little, and then asked if he might leave it an open question for that night, as he hardly knew what his engagements were. And having gained my point I changed the subject, and Miss Rayner's name was not mentioned again.

We had a pleasant evening with our guest. And when he had gone Philip turned to me.

'I need not ask you how you like him,' he said, with an amused sparkle in his eye; 'I never saw my little wife more determined on making acquaintance with any of my friends, or of improving the opportunity. Who else is to be invited to your dinner-party on Friday, may I ask?'

'You mustn't tease me,' I rejoined,' for you don't know my motives. Come and sit down here, and let me tell you all about it.'

He did not seem as interested in my story as I was, though he laughed at my 'match-making' propensity, as he called it.

'I recollect now,' he said, 'that he was engaged to some girl at the time I first knew him. It is strange that it should have been to Miss Rayner. I remember how glad I was when he told me it was broken off, for I feared she would be a stumbling-block to him. I should let matters alone if I were you, little woman. They are very happy now, both of them. It's too late in the day to alter things, and neither of them would wish it, I am sure!'

'You men never understand these things,' I said, laughing;

but at the same time I felt very doubtful as to whether my experiment would succeed.

Mr. Ratcliffe did accept for Friday, and now I grew very nervous about telling Miss Rayner. She arrived, and had been two days with us before I could pluck up courage to broach the subject, and it was Philip who eventually did it for me.

'By the bye, Miss Rayner,' he said at breakfast on Friday morning, 'a friend of mine is coming in to dinner to-night. I hope you won't object. Ratcliffe is his name.'

She gave a little start, but answered, 'Of course I have no objection; but I told Hilda I would not be drawn into society whilst up here. I came up solely on business, and when that is over I shall go home.'

She did not ask any questions about him, and I said nothing. When he was announced that evening she and I were alone in the drawing-room. Certainly of the two Mr. Ratcliffe was the coolest. 'We have met before, Miss Rayner, so need no introduction,' he said, holding out his hand.

She took it. 'Yes,' she said, 'it was a surprise when I heard your name mentioned. What cold weather we are having!' and we drifted into general topics of conversation as easily as possible.

There was no constraint at the dinner-table.

Miss Rayner could always talk well, and I never heard her talk better than on this night; more than once I saw Mr. Ratcliffe looking rather furtively across the table at her, but nothing could have been more indifferent than his tone when addressing her.

Then we began to talk on mission work at home and abroad. Mr. Ratcliffe seemed thoroughly at home with this subject, whilst Miss Rayner grew more and more silent. I was longing for an opportunity to leave them alone, and hoped that we might succeed in doing so after dinner, but I could not manage it. When he was taking his leave he turned to Miss Rayner and said, 'Would you care to come down and see over the premises of the East End Mission I am interested in? If you have never seen London slum work, I think this would give you an insight into it.'

And to my great delight Miss Rayner responded in the affirmative. They arranged a time, and tried to include me in the visit, but I declined; and when the next morning I saw the two walk off together, I turned to Philip with a beaming face.

'There!' I exclaimed. 'I consider I have managed that. Now if they don't make it up, it won't be my fault.'

'You are a foolish child,' Philip responded, as he turned round from his writing to draw me to him. 'Why should you be so anxious to bring them together?'

'Because,' I said, as I laid my cheek lightly against his, 'I want them to be as happy as we are, Philip, and I believe they will be.'

Miss Rayner returned from her morning in the East End very quiet and preoccupied. I asked no questions, but was surprised when later in the day she said to me, 'I must leave you to-morrow, Hilda. I have done my business, and am longing to get out of London. It never suits me. I feel as if I cannot breathe here.'

'You promised to stay till the end of the week,' I said reproachfully.

'Circumstances alter cases,' she rejoined briefly.

This did not sound very hopeful. I was silent, not knowing very well what to say. Presently she said, with a short little laugh, 'I am always outspoken, Hilda, so I'll tell you frankly that if you had not Mr. Ratcliffe hanging about this part I might have lengthened my visit. I cannot stand the chance of meeting him again.'

'Why?' I asked innocently.

'Why?' she repeated. 'You know my story, and he will not let bygones be bygones, but insisted this morning upon dragging up old memories that are best left buried. In fact, he wants things to be as they once were, and they cannot.'

'Oh, Miss Rayner, why not?' I again exclaimed.

'Because we are old and grey,' she said, laughing; 'because he has drifted into ways of his own, and into mine. It would be ridiculous and besides I—I should be no help to him. I am such a beginner.'

She turned from me quickly and left the room.

I was perplexed and disturbed. I had felt sure that my little plan was going to succeed, and I was very disappointed at its apparent failure. I knew that she still cared for him, and why she would persist in standing in her own light, and putting such happiness from her, I could not imagine!

That evening Miss Rayner and I were dining alone as Philip had an engagement out. I was a little anxious about him, as he was only just recovering from a bad cold, and made him wrap up very warmly before he went. Miss Rayner said to me at dinner, 'I am afraid your husband's health is a great anxiety to you.'

'It is a little cloud to our happiness,' I said, 'but we are not troubled. I always feel He is in God's hands; I suppose we shall never have unclouded sunshine on earth, and I don't think I would have it so, otherwise we should perhaps lose the experience of "dwelling deep," and I would not wish that.'

'Have you seen Kenneth at all lately?' Miss Rayner asked. 'I heard he was up in town. Do you know, I used to fancy that he was very partial to you.'

I laughed. 'He says he is still; but Kenneth is just Kenneth, Miss Rayner! I look upon him as a brother. He was calling here the other afternoon and brought Captain Gates with him.'

'Was that your friend?'

'Yes; but he got over that a long time ago. He is engaged to a very nice girl, I believe, and told me he was steadying down. I wish he had the real thing in his life; but perhaps it may come yet.'

A short time after dinner I was surprised by Mr. Ratcliffe being announced. Miss Rayner did not happen to be in the room. He looked a little awkward, I thought, and said, 'I meant to have given Miss Rayner a Report of our Mission this morning, and thought I would bring it round, as I understood she was leaving you to-morrow morning.'

'Yes,' I said gravely; 'I am afraid she is. I wish you could persuade her to stay a little longer.'

I have no influence over her,' he said, a little sadly.

Amy Le Feuvre

'But you once had,' I said softly.

'Do you know about us, Mrs. Stanton?' and there was a slight eagerness in his tone. 'How I wish you could help me now! All these years, though I have steadfastly put it in the background, her face—in fact, her *self*—has been haunting me. There has only been one woman in the world for me; and now, when I find her so changed, I thought that perhaps she might—even though I am no longer young—be willing to come to me. Her parting words years ago were, "It is not you that I dislike, but your views; and those I cannot stand." Now she loves those very things that were so distasteful to her, and yet she will not listen to me. I can only conclude her affection for me died out long ago, and is a thing of the past.'

'No, no,' I cried; 'it is not so. I believe you have always been as much in her thoughts as she has been in yours. I cannot quite understand her now. She seems as if she is afraid of letting you see what is in her heart. I should persevere, if I were you, and make her listen to you.'

I could say no more, for the door opened and Miss Rayner came in. I saw from the determined set of her lips, and the distant, frosty tones in which she spoke to him, that she had no intention of relenting; and I knew it was only a cloak to hide her real feelings, and longed to tear it aside.

I tried all in my power to make conversation easy between them. I could not bear to see the troubled, pathetic look in Mr. Ratcliffe's eyes. Miss Rayner was in her worst mood— cynical and hard. She did not seem to care how she was wounding by her words, and I felt she was purposely representing herself in the worst light possible. Suddenly a thought struck me. I knew how music softened her, and quietly taking out my violin, I asked them if they would like me to play. They assented, and moving to a distant corner of the room I began. I think I put all my soul into it, for I was longing the sweet sounds should soothe and soften her, as they had so often before.

I played on. There was perfect silence in the room. She was sitting in the firelight, and he, leaning against the chimney-piece, never took his eyes off her face.

When I at last paused I saw her eyes were moist, and all the hard lines about her face had entirely disappeared. Without a word I slipped softly out of the room, and going into Philip's study, I knelt down and asked that the two hearts and lives that had been so long severed might be brought together again. Then I waited, and the time seemed long before I heard the drawing-room door open, and Mr. Ratcliffe's voice inquire, 'Where is Mrs. Stanton?' I went out, and received a grasp of the hand that I felt for long after. 'God bless you for what you have done for me to-night!' he said, in an agitated tone; and without another word he departed.

I went in to Miss Rayner. She was sitting where I had left her, but no explanation was needed to see from the expression of her face what had taken place.

I just went up to her, and put my arms round her neck.

'I am so glad and thankful,' I whispered, 'and I do hope that you will be happy.'

Miss Rayner did not speak for a minute, and then she said, in a broken voice,—

'You have brought two blessings into my life, child. This present one is big enough, but the other outweighs it by far, and my heart is too full to speak of it. As for Mr. Ratcliffe, I only hope I shall be a help to him now, and not a hindrance.'

Amy Le Feuvre

'It is all right, Philip,' I said, as I met my husband an hour later in the hall; 'they have come together at last!'

He put his arm round me, and said gently,—

'I hope Ratcliffe will be as much helped and blessed by his wife as I have been by mine. I have experienced the truth of this, "He that getteth a wife beginneth a possession, a help like unto himself, and a pillar of rest."'

THE END

Choose from Thousands of 1stWorldLibrary Classics By

A. M. Barnard
Ada Leverson
Adolphus William Ward
Aesop
Agatha Christie
Alexander Aaronsohn
Alexander Kielland
Alexandre Dumas
Alfred Gatty
Alfred Ollivant
Alice Duer Miller
Alice Turner Curtis
Alice Dunbar
Allen Chapman
Alleyne Ireland
Ambrose Bierce
Amelia E. Barr
Amory H. Bradford
Andrew Lang
Andrew McFarland Davis
Andy Adams
Angela Brazil
Anna Alice Chapin
Anna Sewell
Annie Besant
Annie Hamilton Donnell
Annie Payson Call
Annie Roe Carr
Annonaymous
Anton Chekhov
Archibald Lee Fletcher
Arnold Bennett
Arthur C. Benson
Arthur Conan Doyle
Arthur M. Winfield
Arthur Ransome
Arthur Schnitzler
Arthur Train
Atticus
B.H. Baden-Powell
B. M. Bower
B. C. Chatterjee
Baroness Emmuska Orczy
Baroness Orczy
Basil King
Bayard Taylor
Ben Macomber
Bertha Muzzy Bower
Bjornstjerne Bjornson

Booth Tarkington
Boyd Cable
Bram Stoker
C. Collodi
C. E. Orr
C. M. Ingleby
Carolyn Wells
Catherine Parr Traill
Charles A. Eastman
Charles Amory Beach
Charles Dickens
Charles Dudley Warner
Charles Farrar Browne
Charles Ives
Charles Kingsley
Charles Klein
Charles Hanson Towne
Charles Lathrop Pack
Charles Romyn Dake
Charles Whibley
Charles Willing Beale
Charlotte M. Braeme
Charlotte M. Yonge
Charlotte Perkins Stetson
Clair W. Hayes
Clarence Day Jr.
Clarence E. Mulford
Clemence Housman
Confucius
Coningsby Dawson
Cornelis DeWitt Wilcox
Cyril Burleigh
D. H. Lawrence
Daniel Defoe
David Garnett
Dinah Craik
Don Carlos Janes
Donald Keyhoe
Dorothy Kilner
Dougan Clark
Douglas Fairbanks
E. Nesbit
E. P. Roe
E. Phillips Oppenheim
E. S. Brooks
Earl Barnes
Edgar Rice Burroughs
Edith Van Dyne
Edith Wharton

Edward Everett Hale
Edward J. O'Biren
Edward S. Ellis
Edwin L. Arnold
Eleanor Atkins
Eleanor Hallowell Abbott
Eliot Gregory
Elizabeth Gaskell
Elizabeth McCracken
Elizabeth Von Arnim
Ellem Key
Emerson Hough
Emilie F. Carlen
Emily Bronte
Emily Dickinson
Enid Bagnold
Enilor Macartney Lane
Erasmus W. Jones
Ernie Howard Pie
Ethel May Dell
Ethel Turner
Ethel Watts Mumford
Eugene Sue
Eugenie Foa
Eugene Wood
Eustace Hale Ball
Evelyn Everett-green
Everard Cotes
F. H. Cheley
F. J. Cross
F. Marion Crawford
Fannie E. Newberry
Federick Austin Ogg
Ferdinand Ossendowski
Fergus Hume
Florence A. Kilpatrick
Fremont B. Deering
Francis Bacon
Francis Darwin
Frances Hodgson Burnett
Frances Parkinson Keyes
Frank Gee Patchin
Frank Harris
Frank Jewett Mather
Frank L. Packard
Frank V. Webster
Frederic Stewart Isham
Frederick Trevor Hill
Frederick Winslow Taylor

Friedrich Kerst	Hayden Carruth	James Branch Cabell
Friedrich Nietzsche	Helent Hunt Jackson	James DeMille
Fyodor Dostoyevsky	Helen Nicolay	James Joyce
G.A. Henty	Hendrik Conscience	James Lane Allen
G.K. Chesterton	Hendy David Thoreau	James Lane Allen
Gabrielle E. Jackson	Henri Barbusse	James Oliver Curwood
Garrett P. Serviss	Henrik Ibsen	James Oppenheim
Gaston Leroux	Henry Adams	James Otis
George A. Warren	Henry Ford	James R. Driscoll
George Ade	Henry Frost	Jane Abbott
Geroge Bernard Shaw	Henry James	Jane Austen
George Cary Eggleston	Henry Jones Ford	Jane L. Stewart
George Durston	Henry Seton Merriman	Janet Aldridge
George Ebers	Henry W Longfellow	Jens Peter Jacobsen
George Eliot	Herbert A. Giles	Jerome K. Jerome
George Gissing	Herbert Carter	Jessie Graham Flower
George MacDonald	Herbert N. Casson	John Buchan
George Meredith	Herman Hesse	John Burroughs
George Orwell	Hildegard G. Frey	John Cournos
George Sylvester Viereck	Homer	John F. Kennedy
George Tucker	Honore De Balzac	John Gay
George W. Cable	Horace B. Day	John Glasworthy
George Wharton James	Horace Walpole	John Habberton
Gertrude Atherton	Horatio Alger Jr.	John Joy Bell
Gordon Casserly	Howard Pyle	John Kendrick Bangs
Grace E. King	Howard R. Garis	John Milton
Grace Gallatin	Hugh Lofting	John Philip Sousa
Grace Greenwood	Hugh Walpole	John Taintor Foote
Grant Allen	Humphry Ward	Jonas Lauritz Idemil Lie
Guillermo A. Sherwell	Ian Maclaren	Jonathan Swift
Gulielma Zollinger	Inez Haynes Gillmore	Joseph A. Altsheler
Gustav Flaubert	Irving Bacheller	Joseph Carey
H. A. Cody	Isabel Cecilia Williams	Joseph Conrad
H. B. Irving	Isabel Hornibrook	Joseph E. Badger Jr
H. C. Bailey	Israel Abrahams	Joseph Hergesheimer
H. G. Wells	Ivan Turgenev	Joseph Jacobs
H. H. Munro	J. G.Austin	Jules Vernes
H. Irving Hancock	J. Henri Fabre	Julian Hawthrone
H. R. Naylor	J. M. Barrie	Julie A Lippmann
H. Rider Haggard	J. M. Walsh	Justin Huntly McCarthy
H. W. C. Davis	J. Macdonald Oxley	Kakuzo Okakura
Haldeman Julius	J. R. Miller	Karle Wilson Baker
Hall Caine	J. S. Fletcher	Kate Chopin
Hamilton Wright Mabie	J. S. Knowles	Kenneth Grahame
Hans Christian Andersen	J. Storer Clouston	Kenneth McGaffey
Harold Avery	J. W. Duffield	Kate Langley Bosher
Harold McGrath	Jack London	Kate Langley Bosher
Harriet Beecher Stowe	Jacob Abbott	Katherine Cecil Thurston
Harry Castlemon	James Allen	Katherine Stokes
Harry Coghill	James Andrews	L. A. Abbot
Harry Houidini	James Baldwin	L. T. Meade

L. Frank Baum
Latta Griswold
Laura Dent Crane
Laura Lee Hope
Laurence Housman
Lawrence Beasley
Leo Tolstoy
Leonid Andreyev
Lewis Carroll
Lewis Sperry Chafer
Lilian Bell
Lloyd Osbourne
Louis Hughes
Louis Joseph Vance
Louis Tracy
Louisa May Alcott
Lucy Fitch Perkins
Lucy Maud Montgomery
Luther Benson
Lydia Miller Middleton
Lyndon Orr
M. Corvus
M. H. Adams
Margaret E. Sangster
Margret Howth
Margaret Vandercook
Margaret W. Hungerford
Margret Penrose
Maria Edgeworth
Maria Thompson Daviess
Mariano Azuela
Marion Polk Angellotti
Mark Overton
Mark Twain
Mary Austin
Mary Catherine Crowley
Mary Cole
Mary Hastings Bradley
Mary Roberts Rinehart
Mary Rowlandson
M. Wollstonecraft Shelley
Maud Lindsay
Max Beerbohm
Myra Kelly
Nathaniel Hawthrone
Nicolo Machiavelli
O. F. Walton
Oscar Wilde
Owen Johnson
P.G. Wodehouse
Paul and Mabel Thorne

Paul G. Tomlinson
Paul Severing
Percy Brebner
Percy Keese Fitzhugh
Peter B. Kyne
Plato
Quincy Allen
R. Derby Holmes
R. L. Stevenson
R. S. Ball
Rabindranath Tagore
Rahul Alvares
Ralph Bonehill
Ralph Henry Barbour
Ralph Victor
Ralph Waldo Emmerson
Rene Descartes
Ray Cummings
Rex Beach
Rex E. Beach
Richard Harding Davis
Richard Jefferies
Richard Le Gallienne
Robert Barr
Robert Frost
Robert Gordon Anderson
Robert L. Drake
Robert Lansing
Robert Lynd
Robert Michael Ballantyne
Robert W. Chambers
Rosa Nouchette Carey
Rudyard Kipling
Saint Augustine
Samuel B. Allison
Samuel Hopkins Adams
Sarah Bernhardt
Sarah C. Hallowell
Selma Lagerlof
Sherwood Anderson
Sigmund Freud
Standish O'Grady
Stanley Weyman
Stella Benson
Stella M. Francis
Stephen Crane
Stewart Edward White
Stijn Streuvels
Swami Abhedananda
Swami Parmananda
T. S. Ackland

T. S. Arthur
The Princess Der Ling
Thomas A. Janvier
Thomas A Kempis
Thomas Anderton
Thomas Bailey Aldrich
Thomas Bulfinch
Thomas De Quincey
Thomas Dixon
Thomas H. Huxley
Thomas Hardy
Thomas More
Thornton W. Burgess
U. S. Grant
Upton Sinclair
Valentine Williams
Various Authors
Vaughan Kester
Victor Appleton
Victor G. Durham
Victoria Cross
Virginia Woolf
Wadsworth Camp
Walter Camp
Walter Scott
Washington Irving
Wilbur Lawton
Wilkie Collins
Willa Cather
Willard F. Baker
William Dean Howells
William le Queux
W. Makepeace Thackeray
William W. Walter
William Shakespeare
Winston Churchill
Yei Theodora Ozaki
Yogi Ramacharaka
Young E. Allison
Zane Grey